Stress and Coping in Families

Katheryn C. Maguire

polity

First published in 2012 by Polity Press

Polity Press
65 Bridge Street
Cambridge CB2 1UR, UK

Polity Press
350 Main Street
Malden, MA 02148, USA

ISBN-13: 978-0-7456-5074-6 (hardback)
ISBN-13: 978-0-7456-5075-3 (paperback)

A catalogue record for this book is available from the British Library.

Typeset in 11 on 13 pt Sabon
by Servis Filmsetting Ltd, Stockport, Cheshire
Printed and bound in Great Britain by MPG Books Group Limited, Bodmin, Cornwall

The publisher has used its best endeavours to ensure that the URLs for external websites referred to in this book are correct and active at the time of going to press. However, the publisher has no responsibility for the websites and can make no guarantee that a site will remain live or that the content is or will remain appropriate.

For further information on Polity, visit our website: www.politybooks.com

Contents

Detailed Contents

Detailed Contents

Figures and Tables

Preface

It is almost a blinding flash of the obvious to say that stress is a constant companion for many individuals in today's society. Families are not immune to stress, either, with families facing a number of difficulties ranging from the expected (such as the addition of new members through birth, adoption, or the formation of life partnerships) to the unexpected (such as a job loss or the diagnosis of a catastrophic illness). Hamilton McCubbin and colleagues (McCubbin et al., 1980) wrote that when families have sufficient resources available to them, can meet obstacles and make adjustments as needed, and have strong relationships with each other, they are less likely to view a stressful situation as problematic and are more likely to adjust to stress successfully. Family members' ability to communicate effectively and appropriately with each other allows them to acquire these protective factors and helps them survive, or even thrive, in the face of stress, rather than fall into a state of crisis.

In order to understand how families can adapt to stress, it is important that students of family communication read about stress theory and research from both outside and inside the discipline. As someone who teaches family communication classes and studies stress, however, I found it difficult to find a source that gives adequate attention to the vast amount of research in the area. Whereas some of the leading family communication textbooks have a chapter or two devoted to family stress, these books are unable to give adequate attention to the research outside of communication, where most of the theorizing has taken place. One solution to this problem would be to use supplemental texts that examine family stress management in depth from outside the discipline (e.g., Boss, 2002). Yet, these texts seem to treat communication as a fairly simple process in that they hail positive communication as the cure for family stress. Also, they rarely turn to communication scholarship to inform their theorizing about family stress and coping. If they did, they would realize that communication is a complex process which makes it difficult to say, at the outset, that all pro-social communication is beneficial and all anti-social or a-social communication is detrimental when families are facing difficulty.

Another solution to the problem would be to supplement course material with journal articles that explore how messages affect, and are affected by, stress. Whereas there is a large body of research that examines specific elements of the coping process (e.g., communication as a source of stress, communication as a coping strategy), there has not been an attempt to bring these strands of research together into one comprehensive (and accessible) review, which would allow students of family communication to consider the role of messages throughout the *entire* stress process. Such a review may also help scholars outside the field to recognize the contributions that family communication researchers have made to family stress research.

The purpose of this book, then, is to bring together research from a wide variety of disciplines (physiology, family sociology, psychology, communication) to examine family interaction during times of stress. The book is organized into seven chapters, with the first three chapters devoted to an overview of the stress and coping literatures from both the individual and family perspectives. Because most of this work comes from outside the communication discipline, the fourth chapter introduces a communication-based model of the coping process to demonstrate how communication scholars have studied the various roles that communication plays in the process (i.e., as a stressor and symptom, as meaning-making, as a resource, as a coping strategy, and as an outcome). The final three chapters examine family stress within three specific contexts: geographic separation (Chapter 5), catastrophic illness (Chapter 6), and the transition to parenthood (Chapter 7). I chose these three contexts for a number of reasons. First, all three situations can be considered major life events that happen in the family life cycle, with varying degrees of influence on family life, depending on the circumstances (Miller & Rahe, 1997). Second, communication and family scholars (e.g., Stafford, 2005; Stamp, 1994; Huston & Vangelisti, 1995) have documented both positive and negative outcomes in terms of relationship quality, psychological health, and physical well-being for families who experience each of these situations. Third, communication strategies and coping resources have also been studied within each of these situations, providing a body of research from which to draw (e.g., Bergen, Kirby, & McBride, 2007; Maguire & Sahlstein, in press; Pistrang & Barker, 2005; Sherman & Simonton, 2001). I included extended case studies at the end of each chapter to provide an opportunity for readers to apply the material presented in the first part of the book. Although these cases are fictional, I have based each one on stories and narratives from existing research, my own personal and professional experiences, and stories that friends, family, and colleagues have shared with me.

Acknowledgments

Social support is a key to overcoming obstacles and achieving major goals in life; this is no less the case when writing a book. First, I would like to thank Andrea Drugan, Lauren Mulholland, and Susan Beer with Polity Press for their help in ushering me through the publishing process, Denise Vultee, my local editor, for helping to make the book readable to others, and two anonymous reviewers for their invaluable suggestions. I would also like to thank Mark Knapp and Anita Vangelisti for their guidance when I started developing these ideas many years ago. Additionally, I want to express appreciation to Erin Sahlstein, my co-author on the military wives project, who has encouraged me to reach this moment in time. Likewise, thanks to Loraleigh Keashley, Pradeep Sopory, Terry Kinney, and Matt Seeger for their insightful comments as I continue to theorize about communication, stress, and coping, and to Wayne State University for giving me a sabbatical to work on the book. Finally, I extend sincere appreciation to all the people who shared their stories with me – their words gave life to the case studies included in this book.

There are other people I would like to thank for their instrumental, spiritual, emotional, and appraisal support throughout this process. First, I extend my love and appreciation to my family, John Maguire II and III, Chris Maguire, Patty Maguire Meadows, Miriam Myers, Lisa Lloyd, and Lee Lloyd, for being there when I needed them in the writing process, and to my late mother, Lynn Maguire, for inspiring me to study stress and

Acknowledgments

coping in the first place. I also owe a debt of gratitude to Hank and Rosemary Kumon, whose weekly play dates with Katelyn allowed me to focus on the book. Thanks as well to my colleagues Rashelle Baker, Sandy Pensoneau-Conway, Donyale Padgett, Stacy Thompson, Mary Dixson, Anne Marie Merline, and Nancy Jennings, for their assistance with the book. Last but not least, I cannot say thank you enough to my husband, Ron, for supporting this endeavor and helping me figure out the art of creating figures, and to my daughter, Katelyn, for making me smile when I needed it most.

Part I

Family Stress Theory and Research

The four chapters in Part I of the book introduce you to theory and research on stressful family situations. In the first two chapters, you will read about classic and contemporary research on stress as well as different stress theories that help explain the stress process. Chapter 1 focuses on the individual, and examines the physiological and psychological approaches to stress. Although it may seem strange to devote an entire chapter to stress at the individual level, knowledge of both the family as a whole and the individuals within the family is needed to understand stress and coping in the family system (Boss, 2002). Chapter 2 explores family stress, starting with a discussion of the term *family* followed by a review of important models that have guided family stress theory and research. In Chapter 3, you will read about the ways individuals and family members cope with stress for better or for worse. Finally, Chapter 4 examines how communication affects, and is affected by, stress and coping in families, and is organized according to a communication-based model of coping in the family system. The chapter also offers an organizational framework to differentiate coping strategies based on their form, function, and level.

1

Stress in the Body and Mind

It is 6:30 a.m. and, as Christine turns to switch off the alarm, she realizes that once again she hasn't slept at all. Between the paper she has to finish writing by next week, the news that her father has been admitted to the hospital for a possible heart attack, and her romantic partner's surprise proposition of moving in together, it's no surprise that she can't sleep. When she thinks about her long list of worries, she realizes that the paper is the least of her concerns – that she actually enjoys writing and looks forward to seeing how the paper will turn out. In fact, working on the paper has provided an excellent distraction for Christine, because it's something she can control – unlike her father's illness, which leaves her full of fear and uncertainty as she wonders what the future holds for him and her family. Although she feels better after talking with her mother about his condition, she still feels guilty for not being with the rest of the family during this difficult time. And to top it all off, her partner's desire to rent a house together leaves Christine feeling both happy (because they've been dating for a year now, and she likes the way the two of them are getting closer) and overwhelmed with all that is going on in her life. It didn't help that Christine's partner was visibly disappointed when she responded, "Maybe. We'll see. Let's talk about it more when things settle down." Christine isn't sure why she said what she did; she typically tries to confront a problem as soon as it arises. But given all that is going on right now, that was the best she could do.

If the stress described in this scenario sounds familiar to you, you are not alone. In 2009, the American Psychological Association surveyed more than 1,500 adults ages 18 years and older, and more than 1,200 children ages 8 to 17, about the stress in their lives. Nearly 25% of the adults surveyed reported high stress levels, and another 51% reported moderate stress levels, in their lives during the previous month. Many of the respondents worried about money, their jobs, and the economy; yet many also said family responsibilities (55%) and relationships (51%) were significant sources of stress. The children were not free from stress, either: 14% of tweens (ages 8 to 12) and 28% of teens (ages 13 to 17) said they worried a lot or a great deal, mostly about their appearance and doing well in school, but also about relationships with peers, siblings, and their parents.

The high percentage of survey participants dealing with inter-personal stress suggests that being in close, interdependent relationships can be difficult. As Afifi and Nussbaum (2006) state, "Families are often the source of our most profound happiness and comfort, and yet they simultaneously function as catalysts of frustration and stress" (p. 276). Indeed, family life is full of both predictable sources of stress, such as work/life conflicts or those associated with developing relationships, and unpredictable sources of stress, such as severe illness in the family. Whereas some of these events may happen suddenly and require a great deal of adjustment, others may evolve slowly over time. No matter the cause, when we experience negative feelings related to stress, we need to find ways to manage the situation in order to lessen their potential physical and emotional costs and increase their potential for beneficial outcomes. For these reasons, it is important to understand exactly what differentiates good stress from bad stress, and to determine how people react in threatening or challenging situations.

Defining Stress

If you ask different researchers to define the term *stress*, you are likely to get a wide variety of answers. Stress researchers work in disciplines as diverse as epidemiology, physiology, neuro-psychology, sociology, occupational health, crisis management, organizational psychology, military medicine, family studies, sports medicine, and communication, to name a few. Some scholars are interested in stress from an individual perspective. For example, a medical researcher may study what happens to the body during stressful reactions, or how stress and physiological well-being (such as the ability to fight off infection) are connected. The work of Hans Selye, Janice Kiecolt-Glaser, Ronald Glaser, and others has consistently revealed that too much stress puts a tremendous strain on our bodies and leaves us vulnerable to both short- and long-term problems, ranging from stomach ulcers and sleeplessness to premature aging or even death. Instead of (or in addition to) our physiological health, a psychologist may be interested in how stress affects our cognitive and emotional functioning, or the extent to which our appraisals of stress influence how we respond to stressful situations. Researchers such as Richard Lazarus, Susan Folkman, and Stephen Hobfoll have provided insight into why some of us thrive during stressful times while others cease functioning altogether.

Other scholars study stress from a more relational perspective, believing we are not isolated in our experiences of stress, but instead are embedded within a larger social system, where our stress affects and is affected by those around us. A family scholar, for instance, may focus on what happens to the family system when it is exposed to different stressors, or what makes families resilient in their recovery from a stressful experience. The research of family scholars such as Pauline Boss, Reuben Hill, and Joän Patterson has shown that families can survive or even thrive after some of the most devastating events if the family system is both flexible and coherent.

Finally, a communication scholar may examine how the messages we send during times of stress act as both a coping resource to help us handle stress and a source of stress for those around us. Although the study of stress and coping is relatively new to the communication discipline, scholars such as Tamara Afifi, Kory Floyd, Jennifer Priem, and Erin Donovan-Kicken are unraveling the complex relationship among communication, stress, and coping to show that communication processes such as affectionate expression influence our recovery from stressful circumstances (for a review of the bio-physiological connection between interpersonal communication and stress, see Floyd & Afifi, 2011). My own work falls into this growing area of communication scholarship; I examine the promises, paradoxes, and pitfalls of communication as individuals cope with stress in their relational lives. We need the work of researchers from all of these perspectives to understand stress fully.

The remainder of this chapter examines stress from the individual perspective, with a focus on the leading physiological and psychological approaches. The following three chapters explore stress in a more relational context, with an examination of family stress theory (Chapter 2); an overview of coping at the individual, social, and communal levels (Chapter 3); and an introduction to a communication-based approach to stress and coping (Chapter 4).

Physiological Definition of Stress

Some of the earliest studies of stress emerged in the medical field from testing on animals. Dr Hans Selye, co-founder of the Canadian Institute of Stress, discovered that animals exhibited the same series of chemical and bodily changes as a result of a wide variety of causes and under many different conditions. He labeled these physiological changes the *General Adaptation Syndrome* (GAS) (Selye, 1936). The GAS comprises three stages: (a) first, with the alarm reaction, the body releases hormones and energy in order to prepare for action; (b) next, in the resistance or adaptation stage, the body recovers from action and restores energy reserves; (c) last, in the exhaustion stage, the body becomes fatigued and overwhelmed from a prolonged or extreme alarm reaction. This third stage can lead to irreparable harm or even death. Although we experience stages one and two frequently throughout our lives, we rarely reach stage three. First responders such as firefighters, for instance, likely experience the alarm reaction every time they answer a call about an emergency situation. This physiological reaction helps them perform at their highest level in a time of need. Firefighters' shifts often last 24 hours or longer, with sometimes broken sleep patterns, which can leave them depleted and completely fatigued if they have had a busy shift. This is why many fire stations schedule firefighters on a 24-hours-on and 48-hours-off schedule, so they can have plenty of time to rest and recover from their stressful jobs. The problem occurs when their bodies are not allowed to recover fully from these demanding situations. Energy reserves become depleted, fatigue sets in, and the body fails to respond, leaving first responders and others in physically and psychologically stressful occupations vulnerable to physical or emotional harm (Guidotti, 2000).

From a physiological standpoint, then, stress is our body's reaction to some change or challenge in our environment. Selye's definition of *stress* as "the non-specific response of the body to any demand" (Taché & Selye, 1985, p. 5) is based on the bodily and chemical changes described in the GAS. The source of some changes in the body are easy to identify – for example, an increase in cardiovascular activity (heart rate) that results from physical exercise. Our bodies' stress response, on the other hand, is non-specific: it is often difficult to pinpoint a single reason for it. According to Selye (1993), "a variety of dissimilar situations – emotional arousal, effort, fatigue, pain, fear, concentration, humiliation, loss of blood, and even great and unexpected success – are capable of producing stress" (p. 7). One day, you may feel stress because of a near-miss on the freeway; another day, you feel stress right before you give a major presentation to your peers. Both of these events are examples of stressors, or "any environmental, social, or internal demand which requires the individual to readjust his/her usual behavior patterns" (Thoits, 1995, p. 54). Although each of us may respond differently to a stressor, depending on how we perceive the situation (for example, as a threat to our survival or as an opportunity for growth), our bodies are likely to react in a similar way if the situation is appraised as stressful, regardless of the source.

Figure 1.1 outlines what happens in our bodies during a stress response. Our autonomous nervous system (ANS) governs the

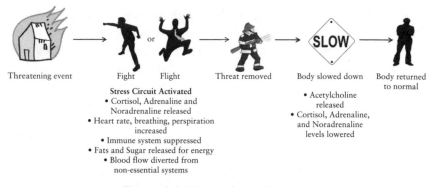

Figure 1.1: Human Stress Response

functioning of the heart, lungs, stomach, blood vessels, and glands – all parts of the body that operate automatically and without conscious thought. The autonomous nervous system comprises two primary parts: (a) the sympathetic nervous system (SNS) and (b) the parasympathetic nervous system (PNS). These two systems work together to create allostasis, or stability in the system. First, the SNS takes over during times of stress; then, the PNS takes over to help our bodies recover from the activation and maintain normal functioning (Campbell & Reece, 2002).

When we encounter a potential danger, threat, or challenge, our SNS takes over by activating the hypothalamus-pituitary-adrenal axis, also called the brain's *stress circuit*, to prepare our bodies for action. During the fight-or-flight response, our hypothalamus, located at the base of the brain, sets off a chemical alarm that tells our pituitary gland to produce a chemical called *andrenocortico-tropin* (ACTH). ACTH alerts the adrenal glands in our kidneys to produce three hormones: cortisol, adrenaline (also called *epinephrine*), and noradrenaline (also called *norepinephrine*). Cortisol tells the body to produce more sugar in order to provide energy to all its parts, increasing our attention span and our ability to process information rapidly. Andrenaline and noradrenaline increase our heart rate and blood pressure to speed up reaction time. Together, these hormones divert energy and resources away from non-essential processes such as digestion, reproduction, and immune response, so that our heart and lungs can function at a high level to allow fight-or-flight action to occur. When the threat has been managed, removed, or reduced, the PNS kicks in to help our bodies recover. It releases a neurotransmitter called *acetylcholine*, which tells our bodies to slow down. As a result, our heart rate decreases, our breathing returns to normal, and our digestive track gets back into action.

When the ANS and PNS work together to handle a sudden, acute stressor, such as an oncoming car or a threatening animal ready to attack, our bodies are able to face adversity, then recover from exertion. When stress is continuous, as is common during times of war or economic uncertainty for example, our bodies may be in a state of perpetual alertness, leading to inadequate sleep, increased blood pressure, and a suppressed immune system that makes us vulnerable to illness (Stein & Miller, 1993). Then again, not all people experience these negative consequences of stress, leaving practitioners to wonder what makes some people more resilient in the face of stress than others. This is the point where psychologists join the discussion.

Psychological Definition of Stress

Whereas Hans Selye was a pioneer in stress research from a physiological perspective, Richard Lazarus and his colleague, Susan Folkman, became leaders in studying stress and coping from a psychological perspective. Lazarus and Folkman (1984) offer two general ways to define *stress* from the psychological tradition. First, some researchers adopt a stimulus approach – in other words, they look at stress as an event that impinges on us. Scholars from this perspective focus on major changes or cataclysmic events that affect a large number of people (such as war or a natural disaster), life events that happen to one or more persons (such as the birth of a child or the death of a parent), or daily hassles or irritants that arise from our roles in living (such as heavy traffic or our partner's habit of drinking milk straight out of the carton). Although you will read more about types of stressors later in this chapter, looking at stress purely from a stimulus approach ignores how people respond to stress, which is the focus of the second class of definitions Lazarus and Folkman outline. Lazarus and Folkman advocate this relational definition of stress as it takes into account both the stressor and the meaning we give to a stressful situation. From this perspective, they define psychological stress as "a particular relationship between the person and the environment that is appraised by the person as taxing or exceeding his or her resources and endangering his or her well-being" (p. 19). The relational view takes into account the reason for the variety of ways people respond to stress. For instance, one employee may react to being laid off with severe shock followed by negative emotional responses such as anger or shame; another may shrug off the layoff notice and feel excitement at the prospect of a new career path. Both of these employees face the same stressor; but one interprets the situation as a threat to ego and identity, while the other sees it as an opportunity for growth and advancement.

The appraisal process lies at the heart of the work by Lazarus and Folkman, and has subsequently influenced the way scholars such as Pauline Boss, Guy Bodenmann, and Renee Lyons theorize about stress from a family, dyadic, or communal level, respectively. According to Lazarus and Folkman (1984), "Our concept of cognitive appraisal refers to evaluative cognitive processes that intervene between the encounter and the reaction. Through cognitive appraisal processes the person evaluates the significance of what is happening for his or her well-being" (pp. 52–53). Cognitive appraisals may take one of two forms: (a) primary or (b) secondary appraisals. Primary appraisals determine whether an encounter with something in our environment is irrelevant (the outcome has no implication for our well-being), benign-positive (the outcome has the potential to preserve or enhance our well-being), or stressful (the outcome has resulted in or threatens to result in some harm or challenge to us). When we appraise the situation as stressful, we must do something to manage it. Secondary appraisals, then, determine what, if anything, we can do in terms of the coping options available to us (which will be discussed at length in Chapter 3), and the likelihood that we can take action. The interaction between primary and secondary appraisals shapes

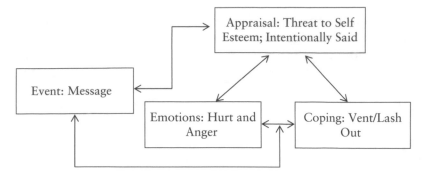

Figure 1.2: The Cognitive Appraisal Process in the Context of
Hurtful Messages
Adapted from Huang and Alessi (1999)

the degree of stress we experience, as well as our emotional reactions to our encounters with the environment. More recent work by Lazarus (1993; 1999) has focused on the association between stress and emotions, and how our cognitive appraisal of a stressful situation can predict our emotional reaction. The research of Anita Vangelisti and colleagues (e.g., Vangelisti, 1994; Vangelisti, Maguire, Alexander, & Clark, 2007; Vangelisti & Young, 2000) on hurtful messages in families provides an excellent example of Lazarus's theory of stress and emotion (see Figure 1.2).

Vangelisti (1994) differentiates between the emotion *hurt*, which is a blend of sadness and fear, and *hurtful communication*, defined as an interpersonal event that happens when people believe they have been emotionally injured by something someone said or did, as when someone is falsely accused of lying or is the butt of a rude joke. The extent to which someone feels hurt, as well as his or her reactions to the hurtful message, depends on how the event is appraised. To illustrate, imagine you are having a nice dinner with your family when suddenly, your mother casually says, "I noticed your pants are fitting too tight and your belly is hanging over your belt. Looks like it's time to start cutting down on carbs and start hitting the gym!" How do you react? The answer to this question depends on how you appraise your mother's statement. If you see the statement as a threat to your self-esteem, because you have been dealing with body image issues your entire life, and you believe your mother made the comment intentionally to upset you, you are likely to feel anger toward your mother and lash out in response. If, on the other hand, you see the statement as harmless, in that your family members have a habit of teasing one another, you may not react at all, or you may even feel loved and respond with a similar teasing statement because you know your mother has your best interests at heart. In both situations, the way you appraise the situation determines not only the emotion(s) you are likely to experience but also the way you handle, or cope with, the situation.

Different Types of Stressors

As is evident in the above discussion, stress is a complex process that can be the key to our survival or the architect of our demise. From a physiological perspective, we respond to stressors at a low level of awareness because our response is an essential adaptation mechanism that has allowed us to survive in a sometimes hostile, unpredictable world: We see an oncoming car heading right for us and swerve to avoid an accident, or we see a vicious dog break free from its leash and prepare to defend ourselves in whatever way is necessary. From a psychological perspective, our response to a *potential* stressor depends on how we appraise the situation. That appraisal can happen consciously and deliberately, or at such a low level of awareness that we might not know why we reacted the way we did until long after the fact. Both of these perspectives suggest that our reaction to a stressor depends, in part, on the nature of the stressor(s) at hand. In this section, you will read about the different ways researchers have classified stressor events and situations. Although a stressor can be classified along a number of dimensions, this section focuses on two dimensions researchers have identified as particularly important distinctions in understanding stress: (a) valence (eustress vs distress) and (b) duration (discrete vs continuous). Two other dimensions – predictability (developmental vs unexpected) and causality (internal vs external) – will be discussed in the chapter on family stress.

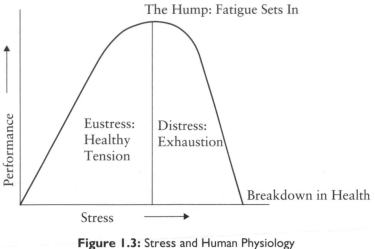

Figure 1.3: Stress and Human Physiology
Adapted from Nixon (1976)

Eustress vs Distress

When most of us think of stress, we usually consider it a bad thing; yet, it has a positive side as well. An examination of the Human Function Curve (see Figure 1.3) shows that increased stress can increase our ability to perform – to a point. Selye (1975) referred to this type of stress as *eustress*; it is also called "good stress" or "healthy tension" because it enhances functioning in our time of need: Stress keeps us safe, helps us reach a higher level, and can leave us feeling excited and fulfilled. Eustress can also come from positive events, such as a wedding: Although stressful, these events are often associated with happy occasions. Once stress reaches a certain level, lasts too long, or happens too often, however, we feel *distress*, the "bad stress" that leaves us feeling exhausted and overwhelmed. For example, in the scenario at the start of this chapter, writing a research paper could be a good source of stress for Christine, particularly if she enjoys writing and research. The surprise proposal from her partner could also be a good source of stress, depending on how she appraises the situation (as a wanted sign of a deepening relationship vs an unwanted threat to her personal freedom). The news about her father's health, on the other hand, could lead to distress if Christine feels powerless to help him and the rest of the family during this time of need. All three stressors combined could lead to additional distress, given that they are all happening at the same time. This situation, called *stress pile-up*, has been linked to problematic coping responses such as binge drinking (Grzywacz & Almeida, 2008), and can significantly reduce a family's ability to adapt to stress (McCubbin & Patterson, 1983).

Eustress. Eustress happens when we have a positive psychological response to a stressor, as when stress is caused by happy events (such as the birth of a child or an unexpected inheritance from a relative) or when we successfully cope with a stressor. According to Simmons and Nelson (2001), "Eustress reflects the extent to which a cognitive appraisal of a situation or event is seen either to benefit an individual or enhance his or her well-being" (p. 11). In their study of hospital nurses, they found that the more hopeful the nurses in their study felt (the more they felt they had the will and the way to accomplish their goals), the better they perceived their health to be. Thus, even in the most demanding situation, we can hold a positive attitude, which has implications for our health. Edwards and Cooper (1988) believed that eustress directly affects not only our health (by improving physical health in the long run) but also our ability to cope with stress by "enhancing individual abilities relevant for coping and/or stimulating increased effort directed toward coping" (p. 1449). In addition to its health-related benefits, seeing a stressor as eustress can also help families cope successfully during difficult times. Black and Lobo (2008) cited a positive outlook – characterized by confidence and optimism, a repertoire of coping approaches, and a sense of humor – as characteristic of resilient families.

Distress. Unlike eustress, which can result in positive physical, mental, and relational outcomes, distress can lead to negative consequences in all aspects of our lives. Distress happens when we have a negative psychological response to a stressor (Edwards

& Cooper, 1988), or when we see a negative discrepancy between a perceived state and a desired state (Simmons & Nelson, 2001). In these instances, we often believe the demands of the situation exceed our ability to mobilize personal and/ or social resources to cope with stress (Lazarus & Folkman, 1984). The American Psychological Association (n.d.) reports that unmanaged distress not only interferes with our ability to live a normal life by leaving us feeling fatigued, out of control, and unable to concentrate; it also can lead to serious health issues, such as reduced immune functioning, or worsen existing conditions, such as hypertension or chronic depression. Our feelings of distress can harm those around us as well, posing a potential risk to the health and maintenance of close personal relationships (Lyons, Mickelson, Sullivan, & Coyne, 1998). As a result, those who experience distress must find ways to manage or lessen the difficult situation in order to avoid (or at least minimize) the potential negative physical, psychological, or relational outcomes of stress.

Discrete vs Chronic

If you ask people to list the stressors in their lives, they are likely to mention a wide range of events, such as traffic on the commute to work, a demanding boss, a close friend's battle with cancer, or the unexpected death of a loved one. Of the three stressors in the scenario at the start of this chapter, two (Christine's father's illness and the proposal) happened quite suddenly and will likely have lasting effects, while the other (the paper) has been going on for quite some time but will end in the near future. These events differ in both their impact on Christine's stress level and the length of time they will last. Likewise, when researchers talk about stressors, they often discuss the properties of stressors that shape our efforts to adapt and cope, such as the magnitude (daily hassles vs major life events) and the expected duration (acute vs intermittent/repeated vs chronic) of the stressor (Revenson, Kayser, & Bodenmann, 2005).

Table 1.1. A Sample of Life Events and their Life Change Units.

Event	Score for Men	Score for Women
Death of a Child	103	135
Death of a Spouse	113	122
Divorce	85	102
Birth of a Child	54	71
Separation due to Work	54	53
Marriage	50	50
Property Loss or Damage	35	47
Retirement	48	54
Trouble with In-Laws	33	41
Outstanding Achievement	33	38
Vacation	20	26
Minor Violation of the Law	19	20

Source: Adapted from Miller & Rahe (1997)

Discrete. Acute or discrete stressors involve sudden changes within a short period of time that require varying amounts of readjustment (Thoits, 1995). Whereas some of these events (such as a family of five coping with a child's broken leg) may affect only a small number of people for a limited time, others (such as Hurricane Katrina or the earthquake in Haiti) could be cataclysmic, resulting in both immediate and long-term effects. Acute stressors also have a specific onset and offset – an identifiable start and finish (Karney, Story, & Badbury, 2006). These "eventful" experiences, whether voluntary or involuntary, desirable or undesirable, scheduled or unscheduled, have been the focus of a large body of research, stemming mostly from the stimulus perspective (Pearlin, 1983).

For example, Rahe and colleagues (Holmes & Rahe, 1967; Rahe, 1975) developed a list of life-change events and scaled them according to the amount of adjustment the stressor would require (measured in life change units, or LCUs). Table 1.1 offers a shortened version of the list from the 1997 article, where Miller and Rahe updated the scaling to reflect changes in society since the development of the scale in 1967. At one end of the spectrum are life events that require substantial adjustment, such as the death of a spouse or the birth of a child. At the other end of the scale are both negative events (such as trouble with in-laws) and positive events (such as a promotion at work) that require less adjustment but are still considered life events (Miller & Rahe, 1997). If you were to scale the two acute events identified in the scenario at the start of this chapter, Christine's father's illness would rank in the 70s, whereas her potential new living arrangements would rank in the 40s. These are compared with the most stressful events (the death of a child or partner, with rankings in the 130s) and the least stressful events (taking a correspondence course or committing a minor legal violation, with rankings in the 20s), with marriage at the midpoint.

In a review of the stress research, Thoits (1995) stated that it is "well-established that one or more major negative life events experienced during a 6- to 12-month period predict subsequent physical morbidity, mortality, symptoms of psychological distress, and psychiatric disorders" (p. 54). Although life events are labeled as acute, they could continue to have a negative effect on our stress level long after the onset of the event, or could lead to a cascade of additional stressors resulting from that initial event. For example, a divorce could lead to chronic stress resulting from loneliness as well as daily hassles stemming from coordinating schedules for shared custody of children (Wilcox, 1986). Indeed, these life events do not happen in isolation from the stressors of day-to-day life. It is the additive effect of life events and chronic stressors that may be most damaging to individuals and families alike (Thoits, 1995).

Chronic. Whereas researchers often like to focus on acute stressors because it is easy to pinpoint their start date, chronic or continuous stress also has the potential for long-lasting and negative physical, psychological, or relational consequences (Boss, 2002; Pearlin, 1983). Continuous stressors are ongoing problems that permeate our daily lives (Serido, Almeida, & Wethington, 2004). They are the persistent or recurring demands that require adjustments over a prolonged period, and often result from individual sources (such as alcoholism or diabetes), environmental sources (such as living in a dangerous area or a constantly noisy environment), occupational sources (such as low job security or time pressure), relational sources (such as domestic abuse), or sociological sources (such as poverty or racial discrimination). These stressors are sometimes considered "background stress" because they are characteristics of the environment: Although their effects might not always be felt, their presence is still there (Gump & Matthews, 1999). When the timing and resolution of the stressor are uncertain or ambiguous, chronic strains may become particularly problematic (Serido et al., 2004).

Thoits (1995) identified two types of continuous stressors that differ in terms of magnitude: (a) hassles and (b) chronic strains. Hassles are the relatively minor annoyances or irritants that happen over the course of a day to disrupt daily life and require only small readjustments. Examples include work deadlines, caring for children, broken appliances, or a traffic-filled commute to work (Serido et al., 2004). Chronic strains, on the other hand, are of larger magnitude and often drain our coping resources, leaving us more vulnerable to the negative effects of stress. For instance, Hay, Meldrum, and Mann (2010) identified both face-to-face and cyber bullying as significant sources of strain for adolescents that can lead to greater incidences of deviance, self-harm, or suicidal ideation. The effect may be greater for cyber bullying, given that the hurtful messages can be disseminated via the Internet to a wider audience and the victim can be exposed to the messages repeatedly over time, even when physically isolated from the victim. Wheaton (1997) identified nine other forms of chronic stress: threats, demands, structural constraints, complexity, uncertainty, conflict, restriction of choice, under-reward, and resource deprivation. Compared with the major life events detailed above, these taken-for-granted hassles and chronic strains may be equally predictive of stress-related physical or psychological symptoms (Lazarus & Folkman, 1984), if not more predictive, because we may have little control over resolving the stressor.

Summary

In this chapter, you read about stress from the perspective of the individual, and learned how stressors could have either negative or positive influences on our well-being, depending on our appraisal of the situation and the nature of the stressor. From a physiological standpoint, the stress response is an important adaptive mechanism that has helped humans survive in an uncertain world. Although a certain amount of stress is necessary for human functioning, too much stress can lead to problems with our physical and/or emotional health. From a psychological standpoint, stress results from a perception that a stressor has harmed or has the potential to harm us or our loved ones. In this regard, the same stressor may be appraised as a harm by one person but an opportunity by another. You also read about different types of stressors and the implications these variations have for our stress level. Whereas we may seek out eustress, or "good" stress, because it often results in positive outcomes such as feelings of competence or resilience, distress, or "bad" stress, causes us to feel fatigued or defeated, particularly when we appraise the demands of the situation as exceeding our available resources and ability to cope. In addition, although acute stressors can have a significant impact on our well-being, they often happen in the presence of other ongoing or chronic stressors that can heighten the effects of stress, which can subsequently affect our relationships with loved ones. The next chapter builds on this research to explore stress in the family system. The chapter not only discusses how families experience and adapt to stressors in their environment, but also the types of stressors that families face, with a focus on the developmental stressors that occur over the course of the family lifecycle.

2

Stress and the Family

It is 9:00 p.m., and Christine has just hung up the phone after her weekly conversation with her parents. Instead of talking with both parents, however, she spoke with just her mother, because her father is still recovering from quadruple by-pass surgery, resulting from years of high-fat eating and low-exercise living. Christine thinks about her parents and all they have lived through – being in a long-distance relationship for the first five years they were together, raising two children while maintaining two careers, caring for aging parents, recovering from a house fire that took almost everything they owned, and now dealing with her father's illness, which will likely result in major changes to their lives. Instead of looking at all of these situations as stress-ful, Christine's parents call them "opportunities" for growth and change, which helps Christine and her sister feel that every-thing is going to work out. Indeed, instead of driving the family apart, each "opportunity" seems to bring them closer together. Christine has learned a lot from her parents; she only wishes her sister handled stress in the same way. Whereas Christine likes to confront problems head-on and work in concert with those around her to solve the problems, her sister seems to prefer talking about feelings and all the worst-case scenarios that could occur. Christine almost dreads calling her sister because she knows she will likely leave the conversation feeling worse – not better – about her family's situation. Nevertheless, she *is* Christine's sister, so Christine picks up the phone and calls her to talk about how they can best help their parents now and in the future.

Like it or not, stress and family life appear to go hand in hand. Afifi and Nussbaum (2006) capture the paradoxical nature of families when they write, "Family members are the people with whom we share our most intimate lifelong experiences. Yet, it is often because of these shared, enduring connections that stress manifests itself" (p. 276). According to sociologist Leonard Pearlin (1983), when we interact with our families, stress can emerge in a number of ways. First, families can be a source of emotional or even physical pain and suffering. Anita Vangelisti and colleagues (Vangelisti et al., 2007), for example, theorized that some families may develop a hurtful family environment characterized by aggression (when family members put down, control, or emotionally damage one another), lack of affection (when family members fail to express positive affect toward one another, physically or verbally), neglect (when family members ignore or disregard one another), or even violence (when abusive behaviors make the environment unsafe for family members). Such an environment could lead to lower self-esteem, increased verbal hostility toward others, higher levels of anxiety, and lower levels of family satisfaction and trust.

Second, even when they are not part of a hurtful family environment, family interactions can still be stressful, particularly during transitional times when roles are strained (as when couples cohabit, marry, or become parents), or when children begin to challenge parental authority. In particular, adolescents' ability to challenge their parents and renegotiate their role in the family is an important, though stressful, step in their becoming autonomous individuals – a step they can best accomplish in a close, supportive environment (Noller, 1995). Although Pearlin (1983) believes that "scheduled," transitional events like the transition to adolescence are not all that problematic because people can prepare for them in advance, family scholars such as Pauline Boss (2002) recognize that any change in the family system can lead to stress.

Third, family provides an environment where we can express and act on the stress we experience in other places. For instance, a parent might pick a fight with a partner or a child as a way to release pent-up frustrations left over from a long work day. Although it is a coping strategy, this "spillover" effect – whereby the stress from one domain carries over to another – leads to problems such as increased conflict with family members, which in turn can leave us feeling even more exhausted emotionally (Leiter & Durup, 1996).

Finally, on a more positive note, family also serves as an important coping resource as we face stressful situations in our personal and relational lives. Gardner and Cutrona (2004) define *social support* in the family as communication behavior that is "responsive to another's needs and serves the functions of comfort, encouragement, reassurance or caring, and/or the promotion of effective problem solving through information or tangible assistance" (p. 495). Whether this communication occurs between partners, parents and children, siblings, or extended family networks, social support is one of the most important functions family interaction fulfills.

The present chapter continues the discussion from Chapter 1 by examining stress in the family system. Instead of focusing on the individual, this chapter looks at the family as a whole, reviewing theory and research related to how family units experience and adapt to stressors in their environment. The chapter begins with a discussion of the term *family* and presents the definition of *family* that will be used throughout the book. Next, you will read about General Systems Theory (GST), a leading theory scholars use to study family life. Then, you will discover how family stress theory has evolved, starting with the ground-breaking research of Reuben Hill (1949) and his ABC-X Model of Family Crisis, followed by Hamilton McCubbin and Joän Patterson's (1983) extension of Hill's work into the Double ABC-X Model of Adjustment and Adaptation, as well as Pauline Boss's (1988; 2002) Contextual Model of Family Stress. At the end of this discussion, you will read about the types of stressors families face, depending on the stressor's place in the family lifecycle (developmental vs unpredictable) as well as its locus of causality (internal vs external).

Defining Family

Although the word *family* might seem simple to define, the term is actually quite complicated and emotionally loaded. The word *family*, first recorded in the fifteenth century, derives from the Latin words *familia* (household) and *famulus* (servant). It was not until the 1600s that the word *family* began taking on the more modern meaning of "those connected by blood" (*Online Etymology Dictionary*, n.d.). A look at different dictionary definitions of the word *family* also shows that genetics and cohabitation are important characteristics of a family:

- The body of persons who live in one house or under one head, including parents, children, servants, etc.

  (*Oxford English Dictionary*, n.d.)

- A group of individuals living under one roof and usually under one head.

  (*Merriam Webster Dictionary*, n.d.)

- A group of people who are related to each other, such as a mother, a father, and their children.

  (*Cambridge Online Dictionary*, n.d.)

The US Census Bureau also includes in its definition of *family* those members who join a family through legal means: "A group of two or more people who reside together and who are related by birth, marriage, or adoption" (http://factfinder. census.gov/home/en/epss/glossary_f.html). Taking these definitions together, we might conclude that a *family* consists of a group of individuals, bound by blood or law, who live together in the same household.

But defining a family on the basis of cohabitation, biology, and/or the law reveals biases that leave many individuals feeling left out of the family discussion. First, the definition assumes that members of a family must live together in the same household.

A look at the divorce rate and the number of children who live in blended families or share time in multiple households quickly challenges this assumption. According to the 2009 US Census Bureau's look at the American family, 68% of all children lived with two adults who were married to one another; 6.8% lived in a household with the father but no mother present, 24.4% live in a household with the mother but no father present; and 6.6% lived in a household headed by a grandparent. Second, the definitions assume that members of a family must be legally or biologically related to one another. Once again, the Census data from 2009 reveal several family types that do not fall into this category, with 6.5% of children living in a household with an unmarried partner of the householder present; and another 1.8% of children living with a foster child or some other unrelated child. With so many households falling outside the traditional definition of a family, it is important to expand the definition to include the myriad family types that exist as a result of forces beyond biology or the law.

The Family as a Matter of Perception

To address the problems with the traditional definition of *family*, scholars have offered alternative definitions that bypass the structural view of family in favor of the perceptions of family members themselves. According to Fitzpatrick and Caughlin (2002), what unites these "transactional process" definitions is the idea that family members are interdependent, committed to one another, and bound by mutual ties of loyalty; they also share a sense of home, group identity, and joint history. Likewise, Pauline Boss (2002) defines a family as "a continuing system of interacting persons bound together by processes of shared rituals and rules even more than by shared biology" (p. 18). This definition clearly implies that the family must have both a shared history, bound by rituals and rules that have evolved over time, and expectations of a future in which personalities will interact and mutually influence one another in the years to come. Galvin, Bylund, and Brommel (2008) similarly define *family* as networks of people who share their lives over long periods of time, bound by ties of marriage, blood, law, or commitment, legal or otherwise, who consider themselves a family and who share a significant history and anticipated future of functioning in a family relationship.

(p. 6)

Their definition is meant to encompass different types of family systems, ranging from the two-parent biological family to committed partnerships with or without children. Turner and West (2006) offer a succinct definition of family which will be used in this book: *A family is a self-defined group of intimates who create and maintain themselves through their own interactions and their interactions with others* (p. 9). As with the other definitions, this definition is sufficiently abstract to include a wide variety of family types, but specific enough to delineate the essential characteristics of a family: intimacy, a sense of group identity, and interaction.

First, *intimacy* implies that the family members are interdependent, meaning that they influence one another's thoughts, feelings, and behaviors. Interdependence allows family members not only to support one another in times of crisis, but also to pick up on one another's stress, because what affects one part of the family unit can affect the others. The term *intimacy* also implies that the family members are committed to continuing the family bond into the future (Fitzpatrick & Caughlin, 2002). Indeed, strong bonds of coherence and a commitment to one another are key factors in what makes a family resilient in the face of stress (Black & Lobo, 2008). Second, *a sense of group identity* is necessary to create boundaries that delineate who is a member of a family and who is not. Families often construct and negotiate group identity through symbolic activities such as family storytelling, wherein family members communicate their norms, values, goals, and culture to others both inside and outside the family (Koenig Kellas, 2005). Although a strong sense of group identity can help families cope with stress by giving them a shared sense of purpose and allowing them to pool their resources to face stressors, too much group identity can stifle individual family members and may prevent the family from turning to outside resources in the face of difficulty

(Galvin et al., 2008). Third, *interaction* is at the heart of family life. As Fitzpatrick and Caughlin (2002) state, communication is "the major vehicle in establishing levels of interdependence and commitment, forming ties of loyalty and identity, and transmitting a sense of family identity, history, and future" (p. 729). As will become evident throughout the remainder of this book, communication and family interaction are at the heart of how families appraise and react to stressors in the family lifecycle.

The Family as a System

The transactional definition of family presented in the previous section points to another important principle of family life that has influenced family scholarship both inside and outside the communication discipline: the family as a system. In 1926, sociologist Ernest Burgess described a family as a "unit of interacting individuals," thus placing family communication in the foreground as the glue that binds a family together. Burgess goes on to say, "By unit of interacting personalities is meant a living, changing, growing thing . . . the actual unity of family life has its existence not in any legal conception, nor in any formal contract, but in the interaction of its members" (p. 5). Since that time, the family systems perspective has become a foundation for theorizing about family stress.

According to Galvin, Dickson, and Marrow (2006), a system is "a set of components that interrelates with one another to form a whole. When individuals come together to form relationships, the result is larger and more complex than the sum of the individuals, or components" (pp. 311–312). Families, as Boss (2002) describes them, "are living organisms . . . the collection of family members is not only a specific number of people but also an aggregate of particular relationships and shared memories, successes, failures, and aspirations" (p. 21). Galvin and colleagues (2006) go on to outline seven characteristics commonly associated with family systems theory:

• Interdependence, where a change in one part of the system affects the entire system;

- Wholeness, where the family has its own unique characteristics that emerge from the interaction of its members;
- Patterns/Regularities, where communication rules and rituals make life predictable and manageable for family members;
- Interactive Complexity, where cause and effect associations are difficult to pinpoint because each action simultaneously triggers new behaviors and responds to a previous behavior;
- Openness, where families permit interchanges with the surrounding environment to manage growth and change;
- Complex Relationships, where families are organized into many interpersonal subsystems of two or more persons, and the interactions between and among them; and
- Equifinality, where families are considered to be goal-oriented, and where goals can be accomplished in many different ways.

(pp. 311–314)

The systems perspective helps scholars recognize not only how stress that affects a single individual can influence the rest of the family unit, but also how the stress the family experiences differs from the stress the individual experiences, and how the family adjusts and adapts to the stressors it faces.

To illustrate, in the scenario at the start of this chapter, Christine's father's illness is not his alone. Instead, as interdependence would predict, it affects all the members of Christine's family. When they first received the news that her father would need open-heart surgery, Christine and her sister fought, as usual, about how best to help the family (a communication ritual brought about by their complex relationship with each other): Christine wanted to do research and read books about the diagnosis and prognosis of heart disease, while her sister wanted to get everyone together to share their feelings about the situation and support one another in this time of need. Christine blamed the fight on her sister's tendency to be over-emotional, and her sister blamed it on Christine's tendency to be hyper-analytical (an example of interactive complexity). The nurse working with Christine's mother suggested that the old ways of doing things would have to change, and developed an action plan with Christine's mother (an indication of openness) to help her father adapt to his new lifestyle by throwing out all the high-fat and high-salt foods in the house and replacing them with heart-healthy options. Without thinking much about it, Christine followed suit and changed her own diet to help support her parents. In the end, Christine, her sister, and her mother came together to address the problem by creating a new mealtime ritual that the whole family would enjoy as they support her father's new lifestyle (an example of wholeness): a family walk after sharing a healthy meal together. As a family, everyone's ideas came together to support a healthy lifestyle for each member of the family (an example of equifinality).

Theoretical Approaches to the Study of Family Stress

The study of stress in the family has a long history, dating back to the writings of Robert Cooley Angell (1936) and Ruth Cavan and Katherine Ranck (1938) on the Great Depression and family life. These early studies stem from the interactional approach to family scholarship, which focuses on the meaning-making activities of the family, an idea borrowed from Herbert Mead's Chicago School of symbolic interactionism (Hill & Hansen, 1960). The three models highlighted in this section build on the work of these early pioneers and borrow heavily from family systems theory to highlight the interaction among potential stressors, the meaning-making activities of the family, family resources for coping with stress, and possible outcomes of the stress process.

ABC-X Model of Family Crisis

Modern family stress theory began with the research of sociologist Reuben Hill (1949; 1958) and his examination of how families coped with separation and reunion during the Second World War. He recognized that not all families experience crises when faced with the same external event: Some families may fall apart completely, while other families are able to cope with the situation and emerge stronger than before. Hill identified three variables that determine why some families thrive while others falter in the face of stress:

> (a) the hardships of the situation or event itself, (b) the resources of the family, its role structure, flexibility, and previous history with crisis, and (c) the definition the family makes of the event; that is, whether family members treat the event as *if it were* or *as if it were not* a threat to their status, their goals, and objectives.
>
> (p. 9)

These three variables became the anchor points for his ABC-X Theory of Family Crisis:

> A (the event) → interacting with (B) (the family's crisis-meeting resources) → interacting with C (the definition the family makes of the event) → produces X (the crisis). (p. 141)

The A factor involves both the stressor event and any perceived hardships brought on by the stressor. For example, a primary stressor event in the story at the start of the chapter is Christine's father's heart condition, a discrete event with a definitive start date that would likely have short-term effects (such as the need for Christine's mother to take on the roles and tasks her father performed prior to the attack) as well as long-term effects (such as the needed changes in eating and exercise habits to help sustain his recovery). Although Christine's mother may find these changes demanding because she has a full-time job and her own household duties to perform, she perceives that she can handle the added burden given what she has been through and the support she anticipates getting from her children, friends, and family.

This leads to the B factor, or the crisis-meeting resources the family possesses, which determine whether or not the family will experience a full-blown crisis. Among the important factors Hill (1949) found in his research are previous success in meeting family crises, the presence of emotional interdependence and unity, strong affectional ties among family members, egalitarian patterns of control and decision making, and acceptance of family members in performing family duties. If a family has the resources it needs to face a stressful event, like Christine's family does, it is less likely to fall into crisis mode.

Finally, the C factor involves the family's subjective definition of the stressor event. According to Hill (1958), the way a family defines an event "reflects . . . the value system held by the family, . . . its previous experience in meeting crises, and . . . the mechanisms employed in previous definitions of events. This is the *meaning* aspect of the crisis, the interpretation made of it" (p. 145). From this perspective, if the family defines the hardship as insurmountable, then it is likely to fall into crisis mode, even if it has the resources needed to face a stressor event. Going back to the story, the fact that Christine's parents often appraise stressors as "challenges" or "opportunities" rather than "problems" or "difficulties" goes a long way in identifying why they have been able to overcome stressor events in the past without falling into family crisis, or the X factor.

A crisis, which Hill (1949) defines as "those situations which create a sense of sharpened insecurity or which block the usual patterns of action and call for new ones" (p. 9), occurs when a family does not have the resources it needs to face a stressor and/or they perceive the stressor as beyond their ability to cope. When in crisis, the family becomes disorganized – the roles, patterns, and norms that typify family interaction are disrupted, leading to intra-family conflict and strained relations among family members, as well as an inability to work together to face adversity. Once the family hits bottom, however, it can begin the process of recovery by creating new patterns and routines and the ability to look toward the future as opposed to dwelling on the present. When a family emerges from a crisis, it is in a new state of reorganization that will guide future family functioning. Yet, some families may fail to emerge from crisis, and instead remain in a state of disorganization. This is where Hill's ABC-X Model of Family Crisis ends, and the work of McCubbin and Patterson begins, as they attempt to adapt Hill's original model to determine what happens in the post-crisis period or when a family faces additional crises.

Double ABC-X Model and the Family Adjustment and Adaptation Response Model

Whereas Hill's work identified some of the fundamental components of family stress theory, some scholars thought the model fell short because it did not consider what happens after the post-crisis period. Hamilton McCubbin and Joän Patterson (1983) made four major changes to Hill's original ABC-X model to address this issue: (a) adding family stress into the equation; (b) identifying four additional factors that influence family adaptation to crisis over time; (c) separating coping from the family resources factor; and (d) fleshing out the adaptation factor (see Figure 2.1).

First, although Hill's research is considered the forerunner of modern theorizing about family stress, he did not use the term *family stress* in his work, focusing instead on crisis as the primary outcome variable. McCubbin and Patterson (1983), however,

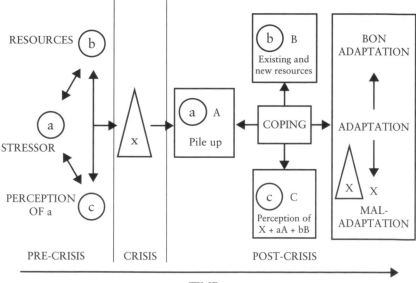

Figure 2.1: McCubbin and Patterson's Double ABC-X Model of Family Adjustment and Adaptation. Reprinted by permission of the publisher (Taylor and Francis Group)

assert that researchers must consider the resulting family stress or distress that arises from interactions among the A, B, and C factors before determining whether a family has reached the crisis stage. Similar to Lazarus and Folkman's (1983) definition of psychological stress presented in Chapter 1, McCubbin and Patterson define *family stress* as "a state which arises from an actual or perceived demand-capability imbalance in the family's functioning and which is characterized by a multidimensional demand for adjustment or adaptive behavior" (p. 9). Family *dis*tress occurs when the family appraises or defines the perceived imbalance in family functioning as unpleasant or undesirable. If a family is able to meet the demands of a situation and/or define it in a way that maintains family stability, then crisis can be averted.

Second, based on longitudinal studies of families where the husband had been captured or was missing-in-action during the Vietnam War, McCubbin and Patterson (1983) identified four additional factors that influenced how families adapted to a stressor event over time. These factors comprise the Double ABC-X Model of Family Stress depicted in Figure 2.1:

> (aA factor) the pile-up of additional stressors and strains; (bB factor) family efforts to activate, acquire, and utilize new resources from within the family and from the community; (cC factor) modifications in the family definition of the situation with a different meaning attached to the family's predicament; and (d) family coping strategies designed to bring about changes in family structure in an effort to achieve positive adaptation.
>
> (p. 10)

The aA factor was added with the recognition that family crises evolve over time, resulting in the accumulation, or pile-up, of additional stressors and strains. These can stem from a number of sources, including the original stressor and its continuing hardships as well as normative transitions that happen in the course of the family lifecycle (such as the birth of a child), prior strains as a result of previous stressors or chronic stress in the family's life (such as a demanding job), consequences of family coping efforts (such as resistance to a family member taking on a new role), or ambiguity about family structure or social resources. Similarly, the addition of the bB factor recognizes that a family may have acquired new resources and capabilities as a result of emerging out of a crisis situation or a pile-up of demands, adding to the individual, family, and community resources in place prior to the family crisis. Likewise, the cC factor takes into account that the family's meaning-making activities have been expanded to include the *total* crisis situation: the original stressor event, added stressors or strains, old and new resources, and estimates of what needs to be done to bring the family back into stability.

Third, the inclusion of coping – separate from the family resource factor – suggests that the family's behavioral and cognitive activities also influence its ability to adjust after crisis. These coping efforts could be directed at managing the problem, maintaining the family's integrity and morale, eliminating or avoiding stressors and strains, acquiring additional resources, or changing the family system (McCubbin & Patterson, 1983). It is the interaction of the coping factor, along with the other three factors, that determines the level of family functioning after the crisis has passed (the xX factor). If all goes well, the family could emerge at a level of functioning that meets (adaptation) or exceeds (bonadaptation) that which existed before the crisis situation. Maladaptation results if the family continues to have problems in the post-crisis period in the form of deteriorated family integrity and/or reduced functioning of the family or its individual members.

Last, in their continued quest to understand the post-crisis period, McCubbin and Patterson (1983) realized that the adaptation process was more complex than originally thought. They began to see it as a two-step process – adjustment to the original crisis (the adjustment phase) and adaptation during the post-crisis period (the adaptation phase) – which led them to develop the Family Adjustment and Adaptation Response (FAAR) Model to clarify the post-crisis period. According to Patterson (1988), the purpose of the FAAR model is to show how families attempt to adjust to stressors or demands before they enter into a crisis and, when they do fall into crisis, how they adapt to their new situation.

The adjustment phase is the same as the first part of the Double ABC-X Model, where a family attempts to meet the demands of a stressor with its existing capabilities. This is a somewhat stable period, in which the family resists making major changes and instead makes only minor changes, keeping family interaction relatively predicable. If the family cannot meet the demands of a situation with its existing capabilities, then it may enter into a state of disequilibrium or crisis characterized by disorganization and disruptions in typical family interaction patterns. Patterson notes that this is not a sign that the family has "failed" in its coping efforts, but rather that it needs major changes, such as the restructuring of the family system, to meet the demand(s) of a situation.

During the adaptation phase, depicted in the second half of the Double ABC-X model, the family attempts to recover not only from the crisis, but also from the family restructuring that took place in the post-crisis recovery. The family thus becomes something "new" in the wake of all the changes and challenges it has faced. Although this phase could lead to a similar or higher level of family functioning, it could also indicate continued maladaptation that requires altering or changing family meanings, reducing or managing the pileup of stressors, finding additional resources, and developing new coping strategies to restore balance to the system.

Contextual Model of Family Stress

Hill's work influenced not only the theorizing of McCubbin and Patterson, but also that of Pauline Boss, a family therapist and scientist who consulted with Hill in the early 1970s on her research regarding missing-in-action families. Early on, Boss found great value in Hill's linear model as well as the subsequent changes McCubbin and Patterson made to that model. More recently, however, she recognizes that the linearity of these models does not quite capture the process of family life (Boss, 1988; 2002). Instead, she believes that process is more circular, as shown in Figure 2.2, where the family stress process (the ABC-X Model) is placed in the center, with level of stress included as part of the X-factor, yet still separate from crisis, as in the Double ABC-X Model. Boss

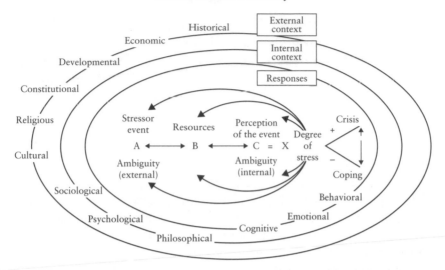

Figure 2.2: Boss's Contextual Model of Family Stress. Copyright 1988.
Reproduced with permission of SAGE Publications

also sees great value in the C-factor of the ABC-X model (family perceptions and meanings). Because she believes family perception and meaning are "central to understanding sometimes puzzling processes in distressed families" (p. 58), she has tried to raise awareness of the role a family's perception of a stressor event plays in the family stress process in her own research on family stress.

Boss's Contextual Model of Family Stress (1988; 2002) is founded on the following six assumptions:

1. Even strong families can be stressed to the point of crisis and thus be immobilized.
2. There are differing values and beliefs that influence how a particular family defines what is distressing and how it derives meaning from what is happening.
3. The meaning we construct about an event or situation is often influenced by our gender, age, race, ethnicity, and class.
4. Mind and body are connected, psychological stress can make us physically sick, and this process can affect whole family systems.

5. Some family members are constitutionally stronger or more resilient in withstanding stress than others.
6. It is not always bad for families to fall into crisis because some have to hit bottom to move on to recovery; those that fall apart often become strong again, even stronger than they were originally.

(p. 15)

Within this framework, she defines *family stress* as an experience caused by disturbances in the family system. Family stress can be either positive or negative; it is a normal, inescapable, and sometimes beneficial aspect of family life. Stress becomes problematic, however, when it reaches the point where the family (or even just one member of the family) begins to feel dissatisfied or shows signs of disturbance (Boss, 2002).

Boss feels strongly that we cannot understand family stress without considering the external and internal contexts in which the family operates. The external context comprises the elements in the environment that the family cannot control – the "time" and "place" of family life. For instance, the family is situated in a broader cultural context that often provides the "canons and mores by which families define the way they live" (p. 44). As such, these cultural meanings likely affect not only how a family interprets a stressor but also how it can or should respond to the stressor, as well as its available resources. Dysart-Gale (2007), for instance, found distinct differences in how North American-trained professionals and Caribbean caregivers view escape from stress as an important coping mechanism during family caregiving. Whereas the professionals suggested that caregivers should get away from the loved one or ask someone outside the family to provide care, the Caribbean caregivers would often turn to family, including the affected loved one, as a way to cope. A family's cultural context could also have implications for available resources: A family situated in a tight-knit community united by a belief in collective action, for example, might feel better able to handle a crisis than a family situated in a sprawling suburb, where the only thing that unites community members is a shared zip code – otherwise, it is "mind your own business." Finally, if a family is from a cultural minority (families of color, targeted ethnicities, same-sex couples), they may experience stress through prejudice, intolerance, and bigotry when living in a hostile environment (Boss, 2002).

Boss believes it is also important to understand the point in history when a stressor occurs – whether it is a past event that has a lasting impact on the family (such as slavery or the Holocaust) or a current event situated in a broader historical climate (such as the loss of a family home during a natural disaster). Either way, the historical context can strongly influence the perceptions and meanings a family assigns to a stressor. Similarly, the economic context can also influence family stress, because it may affect the resources available in a time of crisis. In 2010, the United States was slowly coming out of a major recession, with several states facing an unemployment rate of more than 10% (National Conference of State Legislators, 2010). A job layoff in this economic context would have much more meaning than a layoff during better times, when it might be easier to get a new job. A family's hereditary context can also affect how it interprets and handles a stressor. A family with a medical history of heart disease or genetically linked illnesses, such as certain types of breast cancer, will likely interpret health-related stressors differently from a family without such concerns. Likewise, the interpretation may differ depending on where the family is in the family lifecycle. A relatively young family with preschool-aged children will interpret the diagnosis of a serious illness in one of the parents differently from a family where children are already grown and the parents are retirement-age.

The internal context comprises aspects of family life that members can control; it contains structural, psychological, and philosophical dimensions. The *structural dimension* refers to how family life is organized: the roles, rules, patterns, and boundaries family members create through their interactions. Whereas these structural properties usually keep the system stable, they often need to change to help a family recover from crisis. The *psychological dimension* refers to the family's perceptions of a stressful event at both the cognitive and affective (feeling) levels. Like the C-factor of the ABC-X model, this dimension pertains to the meaning a family assigns to a stressor event, which affects the family's stress level as well as its ability to mobilize resources in a time of need. The fact that Boss includes this dimension again as part of the internal context shows the level of importance she assigns to it, suggesting that it frames every step of the family stress process. Patterson and Garwick (1994) concur, stating that the various levels of family meanings "influence and shape the processes and outcomes of family adaptation to chronic stress" (p. 288). The *philosophical context* refers to a family's values and beliefs at the family level (the family culture). These may approximate or differ from the values of the larger culture in which the family is embedded; when they differ, the conflict can add to the family's stress level. Regardless, these family values directly influence the meaning a family attributes to a stressor event.

The work by Boss and others (e.g., Boss, 1999; Powell & Afifi, 2005) on ambiguous loss provides an excellent example of how the structural, psychological, and philosophical dimensions interact to influence the family stress process. At the structural level, a problem occurs when the boundaries are ambiguous – that is, when a family member's presence or absence in the family system is uncertain. In these situations, the family suffers an ambiguous loss, wherein a family member is either physically present but psychologically absent (as in the case of dementia) or physically absent but psychologically present (as when a family member goes missing). Boundary ambiguity leaves no clear path for action: Roles are confused, the system is immobilized, and the remaining family members have difficulty coping (see Boss, 1999, for an in-depth discussion of ambiguous loss). At the psychological level, family members may experience mixed emotions, or ambivalence, about the loss. This could also lead to family denial, wherein the family refuses to accept the reality of the situation. For instance, when loved ones are missing-in-action during wartime, families may feel unable to grieve because they do not have "proof" of their loved one's death. Instead, families may keep their missing members psychologically alive by believing they will return home from imprisonment. Such a belief prevents families from starting the process of recovery and family reorganization in the likelihood that their missing member never returns. At the philosophical level, if the family belief system leans toward fatalism (the belief that we are powerless to change the inevitable), the family may move more quickly toward accepting the situation, which would allow it to enter crisis mode, "hit bottom," and begin the long and painful recovery process. Ambiguous loss may be more stressful for families that are more oriented toward mastery and control, because there is no apparent "fix" for the situation (Boss, 2006).

In summary, family stress theory has a long and rich history, starting with the work of Reuben Hill and his ABC-X Model of Family Crisis and continuing with the theorizing of Hamilton McCubbin, Joän Patterson, and Pauline Boss. Although the various versions of the ABC-X model have dominated research on family stress, critics of this approach, such as Wesley Burr and colleagues (Burr et al., 1994), criticize these approaches for being too "deterministic" and focused on cause-and-effect relationships (the idea that a stressor *causes* a family to assess its resources, assign meaning to the event, and cope with the event, all of which can subsequently cause a family to feel distress and enter into crisis mode). Instead, Burr advocates looking at family stress as a process with no clear beginning or end – one in which the existing rules and patterns governing family life evolve and adapt to the various "inputs" that regularly enter the system. Boss (2002), however, still finds value in the ABC-X models when they are considered within a circular framework, as depicted in Figure 2.2, which avoids the linearity of the original ABC-X Model and the added complexity of the Double ABC-X Model. Nevertheless, Burr's criticism is an important one, because it highlights the complexity of the family stress process and suggests that there are multiple stressors that can affect families, and multiple pathways families can take when coping with and adjusting to stress.

Types of Stressors

Whether we view the family stress process as a linear or circular pathway, one issue remains salient: the need to understand the nature of the stressor a family is facing. The following discussion of family stressors is similar to the one presented in Chapter 1, where stressors were classified according to the valence (eustress vs distress) and duration (chronic vs acute) of the event. These classifications also pertain to family stressors: A stressor event could produce positive or negative stress in the family system, and the effects of the stressor event could be short- and/or long-term. In this section, you will read about two other qualities of stressors that are often studied in the context of families: (a) the locus of causality (internal vs external) and (b) the predictability (developmental vs unpredictable) of the event.

Internal vs External

When a family faces a stressor, it engages in a meaning-making process wherein it tries to define, appraise, or assess the situation. An important part of this meaning-making process involves identifying the cause of the stressor, because causal attributions can set a "trajectory" for family adaptation to stress over time (Patterson & Garwick, 1994). Yet, as Lazarus and Folkman (1984) point out, attribution is just one part of the appraisal process. For a causal attribution to have meaning in the family stress process, the family must believe that knowing the cause of stress is an important part of its reaction to stress. According to Boss (2002), a family makes an internal attribution when it believes the stressor event began as a result of some individual action within the family, such as addiction, violence, suicide, or taking an out-of-state job. A family makes an external attribution when it believes the events came from someone or something in the family's environment – outside the family – such as a flood, a terrorist attack, or a robbery. Whereas some of these events are volitional, in that the family member wanted or sought out the situation (as when a couple decides to have a baby, or the primary breadwinner chooses to apply for jobs out of state), others may be nonvolitional or not freely chosen (as when a family member gets fired or laid off).

Although there is surprisingly little research on causal attributions at the *family* level, research on attributions at the individual and dyadic levels reveals that they play an important role in how we interpret and react to stress, thereby suggesting how attributions may function at the family level. In a meta-analytic review of the research on coping with illness at the individual level, Roesch and Weiner (2001) found that individuals who blame themselves for their illness were *more* likely to use active, problem-focused coping strategies that, in turn, led to positive psychological adjustment in the long run. In the short term, however, they experienced poorer psychological adjustment. The researchers explain that well-adjusted individuals seek to identify the cause of a stressor – even if it is themselves – despite the short-term consequences, so they can act to manage the problem accordingly. On the other hand, research on marital attributions has shown that distressed couples often make internal, negative attributions for stressful events: Each spouse sees the other as the likely cause of stress in the marriage (Graham & Conoley, 2006). When not distressed, couples make more relationship-enhancing attributions for stressful events that can help them cope and prevent a negative impact on the relationship: Instead of blaming their spouses, they work together to address the stress. From a family systems perspective, then, it may be more beneficial for families to make attributions that avoid blaming a specific family member for stress in the family but instead allow the family to accept responsibility for the situation so it can take action. Indeed, Patterson and Garwick (1994) recommend that families try to construct situational meanings that "reduce guilt and blame and include shared responsibility for managing the condition" (p. 300) so as to increase a family's chance of adapting successfully to a family crisis.

Developmental vs Unpredictable

Many family researchers classify stressors according to whether they occur as part of the "natural" family lifecycle (developmental stressors) or whether they happen unexpectedly or out of sequence from the "normal" developmental pathway (unpredictable stressors; Turner & West, 2006). In either case, the problem occurs when a family is unable to adapt to their "new" reality.

Douglas Breunlin, a clinical social worker and marriage and family therapist, sees family development as a relentless process that is always taking place. During developmental transition points or unpredictable stressor events, however, the process is intensified as families oscillate between the "old" way of functioning that existed prior to the stressor and the "new" way of functioning that is required to accommodate the changes in the family. When the family is able to adapt to the new way of functioning, oscillations are less pronounced and the family can weather these "bumps in the road." If one or more family members remain "stuck" in the old way of functioning, a pattern develops where the family continually switches between the old and new way of functioning for a prolonged period of time; without intervention, the family may never make a successful transition into their new life phase (Breunlin, 1988).

Developmental stressors. According to Carter and McGoldrick (1999), "As families move along, stress is often greatest at transition points from one stage to another in the developmental process as families rebalance, redefine, and realign their relationships" (p. 7). They identify six stages that families go through: (a) leaving home: single young adults; (b) the joining of families before marriage: the new couple; (c) families with young children; (d) families with adolescents; (e) launching children and moving on; and (f) families in later life. Before discussing these stages, however, it is important to note that they represent families from a traditional, structural point of view, with the family lifecycle centered on child-rearing and marriage. Although this model may not represent the lifecycle for all family types, it does reflect the cultural expectations of family life that constrain and influence how families evolve in the United States. Thus, family stress can result not only from experiencing these transitions but also from deviating from this developmental pathway, as when a young adult fails to leave home, when a woman chooses not to marry or have children, or when committed same-sex couples are prevented from entering into legally recognized unions because of their sexual orientation.

In the first two stages, young adults leave home to establish new identities independent from their families and find life partnerships to start their own families. Whereas assuming financial responsibility is part of this independence, many young adults begin this transition when they move out of the house to attend college but remain dependent on their families for financial assistance. Other young adults assume responsibility for their education on their own, enter into the workforce, or join the military to support themselves. Yet, this ability of young adults to be financially independent depends on an economy where jobs and loans are available to them. In an economic downturn, young adults are some of the first to experience hardship, often causing them to return to their families for assistance and thus break from the "normal" developmental lifecycle. According to a Pew Research survey in 2009, 13% of parents with grown children said one of their adult sons or daughters had moved back in with them in the previous year, a common pattern during times of economic recession (Wang & Morin, 2009).

There is also an assumption that the young adult is single and will seek to form intimate peer relationships in search of a life partner. College students who hold onto childhood sweethearts face additional pressure, particularly if they enter into long-distance dating relationships (Paul, Poole, & Jakubowyc, 1998). They may face pressure from friends and family to end these early relationships so they can explore alternative partners before they settle down and enter into the second stage: the joining of families through marriage. This stage entails forming a new family system as well as realigning relationships with friends and extended family. This can be a difficult time as couples work out any cultural differences between their families of origin, particularly if the couples are inter-ethnic or inter-faith (Reiter & Gee, 2008). It is also difficult for same-sex couples, given that civil unions or marriages are not legally recognized in the vast majority of the United States.

The next two stages focus on children in the family system, starting with the transition to parenthood, which will be covered in depth in Chapter 7, and then continuing through adolescence. Whereas the transition to parenthood can be jarring for those who find themselves caring for an infant for the first time, the transition to adolescence is jarring for everyone as the family tries to find a balance between giving teenagers the autonomy they need as they move toward independence, and maintaining family closeness and coherence. According to Laursen and Collins (2004), "Increasing adolescent autonomy inevitably alters patterns of self-disclosure, commonly shared experiences, and perceptions of privacy and responsibilities. Yet, even in the face of these significant alterations, familial emotional bonds are noteworthy for their resilience and continuity" (p. 333). Although most families experience increased conflict and diminished closeness during this period, the process is much more difficult and the adolescent at higher risk of negative behavioral outcomes if problems such as child maltreatment, inter-parental violence, family disruption, low socioeconomic status, and/or high parental stress pre-exist in the family before a child enters adolescence (Appleyard, Egeland, van Dulmen, & Sroufe, 2005). Windle and Windle (1996) report that middle adolescence (ages 16 through 18) is the most stressful time in young adults' lives, producing an increase in internalizing and externalizing behavior problems, as well as the onset of disorders such as anorexia and bulimia. In these cases, teenagers may turn to alternative ways of coping with stress – some of which are developmentally appropriate, such as spending more time with friends, while others are more problematic, such as using drugs or alcohol.

The final two stages involve families in mid- to later life, when adult children are "launched" to start their own lives, and family members face their own mortality (or that of their parents) along with the issues that surround aging. Changes in the parent–child relationship are a hallmark of the mid- to later-life stage as parents and adult children develop adult-to-adult relationships that can be challenged when the parent assumes the caretaking role of a grandchild or the adult child becomes a caretaker for the parent. During the launching phase, families continue to expand as adult children find life partners and have children of their own. Yet, as previously mentioned, these same adult children might return home if they cannot support themselves, often bringing their children and asking their aging parents once again to assume the duty of raising young kids. During the first two years of the Great Recession in the United States (2008–2009), for instance, 1 in 10 children lived with a grandparent, and 41% of those children were being raised primarily by that grandparent (Wang & Morin, 2009). Likewise, elderly parents might choose to live with their adult children either out of physical necessity (because they can no longer care for themselves), economic necessity (because they cannot afford to live by themselves), or practical necessity (because they can help take care of the children). Functional impairment (problems with the activities of daily living), reduced cognitive ability, or problematic behaviors in elder parents place an increased burden on family caregivers and may put the parents at increased risk of elder abuse (Lee, 2009). Aging individuals also face the inevitable loss of their life partners as well as a shrinking social network reduced by illness, death, retirement, and/or relocation of its members (Dickson, Christian, & Remmo, 2004). Then again, with longer life expectancy and a higher divorce rate, remarriage or cohabitation is increasing the number of later-life couples who face unique contextual variables (such as health considerations, retirement, financial planning) associated with their life stage (Dupuis, 2009).

Unpredictable stressors. In addition to the developmental stressors outlined above, families often encounter unpredictable stressors – or, as Carter and McGoldrick (1999) describe them, the "'slings and arrows of outrageous fortune' that may disrupt the lifecycle process" (p. 6) – such as an untimely death, chronic illness, job loss, an accident, war, economic recession, or natural disaster. These catastrophic stressors often result from some unique circumstance that could not be anticipated and is not likely to repeat; they are highly stressful because they require far-reaching and rapid changes in the family system (Boss, 2002). They are even more stressful when they happen at the same time as lifecycle transitions or in the face of chronic strain in the family. Indeed, it is the intersection of unpredictable, acute events with chronic stress and strain that can lead to the most problems for families facing a crisis (Thoits, 1995).

In Part II of the book, I offer an in-depth discussion of two unpredictable stressors. Chapter 5 will explore one source of unpredictable stress in the context of chronic strain: a wartime deployment. Studies of wartime deployment have a long history in the family stress field (e.g., Di Nola, 2008; Hill, 1949; McCubbin, Dahl, & Hunter, 1976), and have recently become an object of study for relational communication scholars who seek to determine how families and couples survive and thrive throughout separation during a time of war (e.g., Merolla, 2010; Sahlstein, Maguire, & Timmerman, 2009). Chapter 6 examines what happens in a family when one of the members is diagnosed with a specific catastrophic illness: breast cancer. Research by Hilton, Crawford, and Tarko (2000) documents the changes and challenges that spouses (typically husbands) face as they quickly assume the unfamiliar role of caretaker when their loved one is stricken by the disease. Children are also deeply affected, as they experience feelings of sadness, confusion, and anger – particularly adolescents, who are old enough to understand what is happening, but feel pulled between the need to help take care of their families and the desire to become independent adults (Davey, Gulish, Askew, Godette, & Childs, 2005).

Summary

In this chapter, you read about stress in the family system and how the modern definition of *family* challenges some of the assumptions underlying much of the family research. You read a brief history of one line of theorizing that has dominated family stress research, starting with the work of Hill and his ABC-X Model of Family Crisis, and continuing with extensions of his work in the Double ABC-X Model of Adjustment and Adaptation by McCubbin and Patterson and the Contextual Model of Family Stress by Boss. What unites all of these perspectives is the belief that the family is a living organism composed of interacting individuals who symbolically create the family's culture, meaning system, and structure. Although the theorists discussed in this chapter are outside of the communication discipline, their work provides the perfect foundation for communication scholars to enter into the conversation because they focus on the messages family members send and receive as they experience and express stress within the family system, and as they engage in the meaning-making process. You also learned about the different types of stressors families face, classified on the basis of their locus of causality and their level of predictability, with a focus on the developmental stressors that occur over the course of the family lifecycle. An in-depth understanding of stress and stressors from both the individual and family perspectives is only part of the equation to learning about the family stress process. The discussion now turns toward another part of that equation: how individuals and families alike cope with stress to optimize the benefits, and minimize the negative consequences, of problematic situations.

3

Coping with Family Stress

It is 5:00 in the afternoon, and Christine begins to get ready for her ballroom dance class. Many of Christine's friends laugh when they hear she is taking ballroom dance, but she goes anyway because it provides the perfect way for her to let off steam, relax, and do something completely unrelated to her work and school. She also looks forward to her weekly chat on the computer with her close friend and collaborator. The two of them have an uncanny ability to anticipate what the other will say, which helps when Christine has a hard time articulating her thoughts and feelings about difficult subjects. Recently, they talked about Christine's possible new living arrangement with her romantic partner. In that conversation, Christine realized she is not ready to make such a financial commitment, because she and her partner have not had any conversations about the long-term future of the relationship. Although this is a conversation she should have had with her partner, she finds it difficult to talk about such topics because her partner tends to say, "Let's not worry about that now. You're too analytical about such things. Just live in the moment and enjoy!" Christine has a similar problem with her sister, who wants to talk about feelings rather than solutions, but not with her mother, who taught her to take action with her motto, "Take control of the problem before the problem takes control of you." This mantra works in most aspects of Christine's life, but the problem with her dad is different: What can she do, 300 miles away, to help her dad recover from heart surgery and completely change his lifestyle? She is not used to feeling so helpless, so she looks forward to a good cha-cha-cha to dance her cares away, at least for the moment.

Given that stress is such a pervasive part of our lives, many of us search for ways to alleviate our stress so we can avoid succumbing to the pressure. In 2006, Mental Health America surveyed 3,000 adults to find out how they commonly cope with stress. The number one way the respondents coped with stress was by watching TV, reading, or listening to music, with 82% indicating they use these methods. A majority of respondents (71%) said they talked with friends or family members to cope with stress; many used prayer and meditation (62%) or exercise (55%). A smaller number of respondents said they ate (37%), drank, smoked, or used drugs (26%), took prescription medications (12%), or hurt themselves (1%) to help them with their stress. This is just a small sampling of the ways we cope with stress, leaving out the more solution-oriented actions we can take to eliminate or minimize stress, as well as those strategies we enact with other people as we join together to confront a stressor. It also neglects the less pro-social ways people cope, such as withdrawing from others or venting frustrations, which can directly affect family members close to the stressed-out person.

Whereas the previous chapters examined the different types of stress and stressors individuals and family systems can face, this chapter introduces you to coping theory and research to demonstrate how individuals and family members manage stressful situations, whether on their own or with others in the family. After a brief review of early models of coping, you will read about Lazarus and Folkman's (1984) Cognitive Model of Stress and Coping, one of the foundational models in the field. You will also read research that situates coping as a social phenomenon with an examination of family coping processes. As with stress theory, most of these approaches were developed outside of the communication discipline. At the same time, all of these approaches suggest that interaction shapes not only the way families appraise stressors, but also how they cope with stress by enacting coping responses to prevent harm or increase the prospects of benefiting from a stressful situation (Lazarus & Folkman, 1984). The second half of the chapter focuses more specifically on coping strategies. Coping strategies can take many forms, such as behaviors, cognitions, or avoidance; they can serve several functions, such as focusing on the problem, managing one's emotions, or maintaining the relationship; and they can be solitary, social, or communal in nature. The chapter concludes with an examination of coping outcomes and a discussion of how even pro-social coping efforts can have sometimes unexpected consequences.

Defining Coping

Researchers Susan Folkman and Judith Moskowitz (2004) tracked the modern study of coping at the individual level to Richard Lazarus's 1966 book, *Psychological Stress and the Coping Process*, in which he first advocated a view of stress that takes into account human cognitive processes. In 1979, Hamilton McCubbin introduced coping to family stress theory with his claim that the family does not merely react to stress, but actively participates in the adaptation process. Since the work of these early pioneers, coping has become one of the most frequently studied concepts in the behavioral sciences (Penly, Tomaka, & Wieb, 2002). A 2010 search of the database PsycInfo revealed more than 5,400 published journal articles, 100 books, and 650 book chapters that included "coping" as a keyword descriptor and cited the research of Richard Lazarus and/or Hamilton McCubbin in the publication. The first part of this section will explore the work of Richard Lazarus and his colleagues in their study of coping from the individual perspective. The discussion will then turn toward research by family and relationship scholars who view coping as a social process that often involves multiple people, as opposed to one solitary individual.

From the Individual Perspective

In writing about the history of coping research, Lazarus and his colleagues describe two models that guided early coping research.

First, studies of coping began with investigations of how animals cope with their environment to ensure their survival (e.g., Obrist, 1981). From this perspective, *coping* is defined as behaviors (such as escape or avoidance) that control the environment in order to lessen any psychophysiological disturbances that might occur (Folkman & Lazarus, 1991). A second perspective, the ego psychology model, was introduced to go beyond the drive and arousal models by including the human thought processes that bring someone to a coping action (e.g., Menninger, 1963). This approach views *coping* as "realistic and flexible thoughts and acts that solve problems and thereby reduce stress" (Lazarus & Folkman, 1984, p. 118). Researchers using the ego model also conceptualize coping as a stable disposition, either as a style (general approaches we use to deal with stress) or a trait (properties in us that cause us to act in certain ways), that persists over time (Folkman & Lazarus, 1991).

Although recognizing the inclusion of human thought processes was an important advancement in coping research, Lazarus and his colleagues have criticized trait or style models of coping as being too simplistic. From these perspectives, "we end up speaking of people who are repressors or vigilants; people who are field-dependent or -independent; people who are deniers, and so on" (Folkman & Lazarus, 1991, p. 195). Furthermore, Cohen and Lazarus (1973) found that trait measures of coping are poor predictors of actual coping behavior in specific circumstances. As a result, Lazarus and Folkman (1984) developed a theoretical approach to studying coping as a process that changes over time and in different contexts. Whereas coping style emphasizes personality traits, coping process emphasizes temporal and contextual influences on coping (Lazarus, 1993).

In their landmark book, *Stress, Appraisal, and Coping*, Lazarus and Folkman (1984) define *coping* as "constantly changing cognitive and behavioral efforts to manage specific external and/or internal demands that are appraised as taxing or exceeding the resources of a person" (p. 141). They prefer this definition of coping to the earlier definitions of coping for three reasons. First, the definition is contextual: It recognizes that our encounter with a situation shapes coping through our appraisal of the actual demands in the encounter and our available resources for managing them. Thus, it is important to understand whether or not the stressor event is imminent, novel, predictable (we can see it coming), and/or uncertain, as well as its likely duration and the degree of ambiguity surrounding it. Second, instead of labeling a strategy "adaptive" or "maladaptive" from the start, the definition treats coping as a neutral concept. Indeed, Lazarus (1993) believes that whether a coping response is adaptive or not depends on the person, the type of stressor, and the type of outcome sought (for example, a decrease in distress). Third, the definition of coping allows for the consideration of how coping may change as our encounter with the stressor unfolds.

Cognitive appraisals are an important part of the model Lazarus and Folkman created. Appraisals occur when we evaluate whether particular encounters with the environment are relevant to our well-being and, if so, in what ways (Folkman, Lazarus, Dunkel-Shetter, DeLongis, & Gruen, 1986). Primary appraisals include perceptions of threat (the potential for harm or loss to our own or a loved one's self-esteem, goals, health and safety, or resources), challenge (the potential for growth, mastery, or gain), or harm-loss (injury already done, as in harm to a friendship, health, or self-esteem). Only when we perceive situations as stressful will we decide to do something to counteract any negative consequences stemming from the source of stress. Secondary appraisals occur when we evaluate various coping strategies we could use, given available resources any situational constraints that exist (such as restricted communication because of geographic separation from our support system) and the "social and personal characteristics upon which people may draw when dealing with stressors" (Lazarus & Folkman, 1984, p. 59). Example resources include health and energy, positive beliefs, problem-solving skills, social skills, and material resources (Thoits, 1995). Secondary appraisals also involve perceptions (a) that we could change or do something about the situation, (b) that we have to accept the situation, (c) that we need to know more information before we can act, or (d) that we have to hold ourselves back from doing whatever we want (Folkman et al., 1986, p. 994).

Consider, for example, two people who have to complete a major project for work. One was given several weeks to complete the project, and has gathered all the resources and help she needs. Although she feels stressed, because failure to complete the project could result in a negative annual review and no increase in pay, she feels in control of the situation and copes quite well, so she can finish the project successfully and on time. The other person, however, was given only two days to complete his project, leaving him little time to get what he needs to succeed. He sees the situation as much more serious: Although the consequences are similar, his limited resources increase his stress level so much that he is unable to think through the problem effectively and starts to panic. He takes a brief walk to the lunch room to grab a cup of coffee and relax for a moment. After that, he remembers that his colleague has a computer program that can facilitate the project, and he asks for his assistance. As a result, he is able to complete his project successfully and on time as well. Both employees felt stress, but their reactions and coping responses varied according to their appraisals of the stressor, the situation, and their resources.

In addition to cognitive appraisals and context, individual differences, or "personality" variables, are likely to exert a strong influence on the coping process as well. For example, Hobfoll et al. (1994) predicted that personality variables such as gender, gender role orientation (expectations about men's and women's roles), and mastery (the extent to which we feel in control of our lives) would affect the way we cope with stressors in our lives. Results indicated that women used social joining (coalition-building with others) and social support more often than men, particularly when coping with relational stressors (such as a fight with a spouse). In addition, traditional individuals ("masculine" males or "feminine" females) used social joining more often than non-traditional individuals. Finally, people who scored high in mastery used more assertive and aggressive action, and less avoidance, than those who scored lower in mastery (Hobfoll et al., 1994). Hope theory (Snyder, 2002) suggests that high-hope people – those who enjoy goal pursuits and engage in them with a positive attitude – are better able to cope with a stressor, as they often appraise it as a "challenge" to be met rather than an insurmountable situation.

Another individual-level variable that influences how we cope with stress is where we are in our lifespan. Compas and associates (Compas, Connor-Smith, Satlzman, Thomsen, & Wadsworth, 2001) reviewed the research on coping with stress during childhood and adolescence. According to the authors, "An individual's developmental level both contributes to the resources that are available for coping and limits the types of coping responses the individual can enact" (p. 89). Whereas some aspects of our response to a stressor – such as crying when distressed – are in place at birth, other coping responses – such as using an object for self-comfort or more advanced coping responses such as using self-talk to calm negative emotions – evolve over time as a child becomes more cognitively developed and acquires new communication skills. In a study of stress and coping among 8- to 13-year-olds, Hampel and Petermann (2005) found that adaptive strategies such as support-seeking and problem-solving are acquired in early childhood, and these strategies do not change over time; but maladaptive strategies, such as aggression, increase with age. The authors suggest that children in early adolescence may be at increased risk for psychological problems if they use these negative coping efforts over the more adaptive efforts in place during early childhood. Similarly, Amirkhan and Auyeung (2007) studied whether there are differences in coping between the young and the old. Their study of pre-teens (9–12 years old), early teens (13–15 years old), late teens (16–18 years old), younger adults (20–29 years old), and older adults (30 years and older) found that although they used the same types of strategies (avoidance, seeking support, problem-solving), older individuals tended to use the more adaptive problem-focused strategies whereas younger individuals tended to use more escapist strategies. The authors explained that these differences are likely due to greater life experiences among older adults, increased biological, emotional, and cognitive maturity, and having more access to a wider variety of coping resources.

Although Lazarus and Folkman's process approach took coping beyond the simple stressor-reaction model by including primary and secondary appraisals, focusing on the context, and separating the coping behavior from the coping outcome, it leaves out two important factors relevant to the study of family stress: the impact of significant others on coping and the role of interpersonal communication in the coping process. Whereas the process approach to coping does allude to relationships and communication in the form of a specific coping strategy (seeking social support), close relationships – specifically, family relationships – play a greater role in the coping process than the individual perspective recognizes. Hobfoll et al. (1994) identified this shortcoming, pointing out that (a) many of life's stressors are interpersonal or have an interpersonal component, (b) individual coping efforts have potential social consequences, and (c) the act of coping often requires interaction with others. The next section addresses these issues by examining coping from a relational perspective.

From the Relational Perspective

Stemming from the work of Lazarus on individual coping, research from a relational perspective has taken two paths: (a) coping in families and (b) coping in couples. Hamilton McCubbin was one of the first family scholars to include coping in his model of the family stress process outlined in Chapter 2. Although he found great value in Hill's original ABC-X Model of Family Crisis, McCubbin (1979) believed that *coping*, defined simply as the use of specific strategies to manage stress, should be considered separately from family resources: Just because a family has resources does not mean it will actually use them. As a result of this change, coping becomes an additional determinant of whether a family successfully adapts to crisis. McCubbin and Patterson's (1983) Double ABC-X model reflects this belief: They hypothesized that coping influences not only family adaptation (the xX factor), but also the other factors (pile-up, or the aA factor; existing and new resources, or the bB factor; and new perceptions, or the cC factor).

The FAAR Model further highlights the role of coping as it influences family adjustment and adaptation.

In her view of family stress theory, Boss (2002) also emphasizes the importance of both individual action and *family coping*, which she defines as the family group's management of a stressful event or situation. Recall that her Contextual Model of Family Stress has three outer layers that surround her adaptation of Hill's ABC-X model: (a) an outer ring representing the external environment, (b) a middle ring representing the internal environment, and (c) an inner ring representing responses (coping). She borrows heavily from Richard Lazarus's work as she outlines the various coping options available to individuals and families under stress, including direct actions that can change or alter the stressful situation (such as learning new skills), cognitions that help reduce the emotional arousal of a situation (such as looking at the positive outcomes of a bad situation), and emotion-regulation behaviors that manage one's emotional reaction to stress (such as journaling). If a family can successfully cope with a stressor event, then it will never reach crisis status. From a systems perspective, however, if even one person is stressed, or if the family's coping response harms a single family member, then the family is not coping effectively, which can lead to crisis. This may not be a bad outcome, because families may need to enter into a crisis situation so they can reorganize the system and develop new rules if current efforts are hurting individual members. For instance, families where one member is an alcoholic often place blame for family stress on a "scapegoat" – often a child who tends to act out during times of stress. In order to accept communal responsibility for their problems and avoid scapegoating, such families need to change the way they interact, because the system is currently set up to "enable" the alcoholic's addiction. This revolutionary change often happens when the family is in crisis and turns to professional counselors for help.

A second line of research from the relational perspective has focused on the marital dyad, starting in the early 1990s with studies of how couples cope with chronic illness. For example, Wethington and Kessler (1991) extended the process approach to coping by including a dyadic component in the model, identifying two ways the actions and reactions of others experiencing the same situation affect our coping process. First, one partner's choice of coping strategy could influence the strategy choice of the other partner by modeling coping responses (social referencing; Bandura, 1986). Second, the way one partner copes with distress could cause distress in the other partner. This process of mutual influence in coping results from interdependence, "the extent to which the needs and goals of both the recipient and provider are apparent in the relationship and the problems of coordination that both parties face in meeting each other's needs" (Coyne, Ellard, & Smith, 1990, p. 138). One implication of this approach to coping is that relational partners may need to coordinate their coping efforts in order to both manage stress and preserve the relationship.

Significant others can influence the coping process in another way, particularly when the stressor affects both people, a process called mutual or dyadic coping. For mutual coping to occur, both partners must agree that the event is stressful to both of them; thus, both individuals share the burden of coping (Wethington & Kessler, 1991). According to DeLongis and O'Brien (1991), "the burden of chronic illness is experienced not only by the patient but also has widespread effects on the lives of family members" (p. 222). Their investigation of how couples cope with Alzheimer's disease not only reveals the ways couples cope together with the illness, but also how the relationship itself can influence the coping process and vice-versa. Similarly, dyadic coping involves "the interplay between the stress signals of one partner and the coping reactions of the other" (Revenson, et al., 2005, p. 4) and highlights the stress communication process, whereby "one partner's stress is communicated to the other who perceives, interprets, and decodes these signals and responds with some form of dyadic coping" (Bodenmann, 2005, p. 36). Dyadic coping strategies, including positive dyadic coping (such as offers of support), common dyadic coping (such as joint problem-solving), and negative dyadic coping (such as support accompanied by mockery), all involve communication (Bodenmann, 1995), thereby placing interaction at the center of the dyadic coping process. Similar to individual coping strategies, the likelihood that a couple will use dyadic or mutual coping may depend on their developmental life stage, in that older couples have more maturity and a longer track record in collaborating together on problems, and thus, may be more likely to engage in mutual coping than younger couples (Berg & Upchurch, 2007).

In summary, the pioneering work of Richard Lazarus in the 1960s paved the way for the study of coping from the individual, dyadic, and family perspectives. Lazarus and Folkman's (1984) process approach to coping closely mirrors the models of family stress that McCubbin and Patterson (1983) and Boss (2002) proposed, in that they all (a) emphasize the importance of context and understanding the nature of the stressor at hand, (b) highlight meaning-making as a critical determinant in the coping process, (c) differentiate coping strategies from coping resources and coping outcomes, and (d) include a time element to demonstrate how the process evolves over time and across different situations. Although researchers agree that coping plays a critical role in how individuals and families manage stress, they differ in how they operationalize or conceptualize specific coping responses (Skinner, Edge, Altman, & Sherwood, 2003). The discussion now turns to an examination of coping strategies through the different lenses used to understand this important concept.

Types of Coping Strategies

Coping strategies are the behaviors we use to manage stress and protect ourselves from psychological harm (McCubbin, 1979; Pearlin & Schooler, 1978; Thoits, 1995). Although the strategies researchers identify differ depending on the theoretical framework from which they study coping (for example, trait vs process approach) or the context under investigation (for example, illness, transition to parenthood, or war-induced military separation), most strategies can be classified according to (a) the property or form of the strategy, (b) the focus or function of the strategy, and (c) the level of the strategy.

Forms of Coping

One of the oldest and most common ways to distinguish different types of coping responses is according to whether the efforts are active and oriented toward confronting the problem (approach strategies) or avoidant and oriented toward reducing tensions (avoidance strategies); (Skinner et al., 2002). For example, Billings and Moos (1981) identified three general types of coping strategies: active-behavioral, active-cognitive, and avoidance. Active-behavioral strategies are overt behavioral attempts to deal directly with the problem, such as actively confronting a situation, exercising, seeking social support, social joining, attending to instrumental needs of the situation, actively engaging in discussions about the problem, sharing meaning, seeking information, negotiating, and catharsis (Billings & Moos, 1981; Coyne & Smith, 1991; DeLongis & O'Brien, 1990; Folkman et al., 1986; Hilton & Koop, 1994; Hobfoll et al., 1994; Holahan & Moos, 1987; Pearlin & Schooler, 1978; Thoits, 1991). Active-cognitive strategies are efforts to manage how we appraise the stressor or the event, such as reframing or reinterpreting the situation, accepting the situation, praying, reinterpreting feelings, and having self-control (Billings & Moos, 1981; Folkman et al., 1986; Holahan & Moos, 1987; Pearlin & Schooler, 1978; Thoits, 1991). Avoidance strategies are attempts to avoid confronting the problem, such as hiding information from our partners or from ourselves; or to reduce tension indirectly by behaviors such as eating, smoking, or taking it out on other people (Billings & Moos, 1981; Coyne & Smith, 1991; Folkman et al., 1986; Holahan & Moos, 1987). Whereas many researchers use this approach to understanding coping, it is problematic because it is often difficult to determine whether a particular behavior is approach- or avoidance-oriented (for example, do we seek support in order to confront a problem or to take a break from the problem?), and it leaves out other forms of coping that do not easily fall into one of these categories (such as observation) (Skinner et al., 2002).

Functions of Coping

In addition to categorizing coping strategies according to form, many approaches distinguish coping strategies according to how, exactly, they are intended to help. In reviewing the literature, there appear to be four groups of coping that differ according to their function: (a) problem-focused, (b) emotion-focused, (c) meaning-focused, and (d) relationship-focused coping (Folkman & Moskowitz, 2004).

Problem-focused coping. Problem-focused coping includes behaviors aimed at managing or altering the problem causing the distress (Holahan & Moos, 1987; Lazarus & Folkman, 1984). These behaviors occur most frequently when we appraise conditions as amenable to change. Problem-focused strategies can be similar to those used for problem solving, such as defining the problem, generating alternative solutions, weighing the alternatives in terms of their costs and benefits, choosing among them, and acting on a situation. Stetz, Lewis, and Primomo (1986), for instance, identified a number of problem-oriented coping strategies families use when coping with chronic illness in the mother, including alterations in household management, in which family members coordinate roles and the distribution of aid to family members; seeking assistance or information from outside of the family household; and mobilizing household family members to take action to address concrete problems the family faces. Problem-oriented coping strategies can also be focused inward such as learning a new skill or behavior (Lazarus & Folkman, 1984). Another type of problem-oriented coping strategy, labeled broad-minded coping, occurs when someone is able to explore multiple pathways to addressing a stressor (Fredrickson, 2001). This type of strategy is facilitated by positive emotions such as love, contentment, and joy: When people experience these emotions, particularly during times of extreme distress, they are more able to think "outside the box" which enhances not only their coping ability but their psychological well-being as well. The identification of problem-focused strategies depends to a certain extent on the types of problems we are trying to solve, once again highlighting the context-dependent nature of coping: The more situation-specific the research domain is, the greater the proliferation of problem-focused strategies.

Emotion-focused coping. Emotion-focused coping refers to cognition or behaviors directed at regulating our emotional response to the problem (Coyne & Smith, 1991; Lazarus & Folkman, 1984). These strategies are prevalent when we appraise a situation as out of our family's control – that is, we have decided little can be done to modify harmful, threatening, or challenging environmental conditions. According to Lazarus and Folkman (1984), "The greater the threat, the more primitive, desperate, or regressive emotion-focused forms of coping tend to be and the more limited the range of problem-focused forms of coping" (p. 168). A wide range of emotion-focused strategies can be found in the literature, including cognitive (for example, avoidance, minimization, distancing, or selective attention) and behavioral responses (for example, drinking, exercising) directed at lessening emotional distress (Folkman & Lazarus, 1985). In the family literature, Burr et al. (1994) identified a number of emotion-focused coping responses, such as expressing positive and negative feelings and cultivating an increased awareness of one another's emotional needs. In the study of family coping and maternal chronic illness referenced earlier, families would also cope by getting away from the situation, participating in activities unrelated to the problem, and talking about concerns with friends and family to manage their emotions (Stetz et al., 1986).

Meaning-focused coping. Meaning-focused coping refers to cognitive strategies we use to manage the meaning of a stressful encounter (Folkman & Moskowitz, 2004). According to Park (2010), meaning-making plays an important role in the primary appraisal process when the appraised meaning of a situation differs from our global meaning (the cognitive framework with which we interpret experiences and provide motivation) – as, for example, when we see a loved one's battle with cancer as hopeful rather than feeling hopeless. Meaning-making also plays a role in the coping process when we attempt to reduce the discrepancy between the appraised and global meanings, as when we interpret a loved one's cancer diagnosis as an opportunity for growth rather than a pathway to catastrophe. Folkman (2008) states that meaning-focused coping in which "the person draws on his or her beliefs (religious, spiritual, or secular), values (such as "mattering"), and existential goals (purpose in life or guiding principles) to motivate and sustain coping and well-being during difficult times" can lead us to generate positive emotions, even during times of stress (p. 7). Examples from the family stress literature include changing how we view or define the situation, believing in God, altering our perspectives, and reframing (redefining a stressful situation to make it more manageable) (Burr et al., 1994; McCubbin, Larsen, & Olsen, 1982; Stetz et al., 1986). Again referring to the study of chronic illness in mothers by Stetz et al. (1986), they found that families would cope with stress by altering their perspectives and redefining the challenge or problem as something manageable.

Relationship-focused coping. Relationship-focused coping goes beyond problems and emotion to how relational partners deal with each other (Coyne & Smith, 1991). Coyne and Fiske (1992) chose the term "relationship-focused coping" to describe the strategies couples use to grapple with each other's presence and emotional needs when one spouse becomes seriously ill. They identified two strategies couples use to cope in this particular context: (a) active engagement (for example, direct discussions with the spouse) and (b) protective buffering (for example, hiding bad news from the spouse). DeLongis and O'Brien (1990) also emphasized the importance of relationship-focused strategies in their study of couples coping with Alzheimer's disease, stating that "Successful coping may depend not only on our ability to keep our emotions under control and our ability to resolve problems, but also our ability to regulate our social relationships" (p. 229). One relationship-enhancing strategy is empathic coping: "attempts to both perceive accurately the affective world of others involved in the stressful situation and to communicate accurately and sensitively one's affective understanding to those people" (DeLongis & O'Brien, p. 230). These relationship-focused responses involve the relational partner either directly, as an active participant, or indirectly, as the focus of the response.

Studying coping according to its function has added much to the coping research. Although this approach recognizes rational decision making, dealing with emotions, meaning-making, and managing the relationship as critical parts of the coping process, it fails to recognize the diversity of strategies within these categories (for example, that social withdrawal, commonly classified as an emotion-focused strategy, can be a problem-focused strategy if the person is the source of stress), or the possibility that certain strategies can fulfill multiple functions at the same time (for example, that working together with a romantic partner can solve a problem and strengthen the relationship; Skinner et al., 2002).

Levels of Coping

A final way to classify different forms of coping is according to the levels at which they take place. According to Skinner et al. (2002), "Some researchers have suggested that an important distinction in categorizing coping is the social orientation of the strategy, specifically, whether a way of coping is social versus solitary" (p. 230). Traditional views of coping see it as a highly individual affair, often done in isolation from others. Researchers who study stress and coping from a dyadic or family perspective, however, have always recognized that coping is a social affair that often involves other people. The three levels of coping that are commonly used in the literature are solitary, social, and communal.

Solitary coping. The first level, solitary or individual coping, closely mirrors the research of Lazarus and colleagues. These are the strategies we enact at the individual level as we find ways to face problems, manage emotions, alter meanings, and manage relational interactions in the face of stress. One of the most commonly used questionnaires to assess coping at the individual level is the Revised Ways of Coping Questionnaire (Folkman et al., 1986), which includes a variety of strategies: confrontive coping (such as expressing anger), distancing (such as making light of the situation), self-control (such as keeping feelings to ourselves), seeking social support, accepting responsibility, escape-avoidance (such as drinking), planful problem-solving (such as making and following a plan of action), and positive reappraisal (such as finding new faith). In family stress research, studies on separation in the family consistently identify two coping patterns the mother employs to help the family adapt to a father's absence: (a) establishing independence and self-sufficiency, and (b) maintaining family integrity (Boss, 2002). Examples from more recent military family research include acceptance, planning, self-distraction, self-blame, and denial (Dimiceli, Steinhardt, & Smith, 2010). Although we enact each of these strategies at the individual level, relationship and family researchers recognize that they can affect those around us: Expressing anger may be directed at a loved one; executing a plan may require the assistance of others; and maintaining family integrity involves bringing loved ones together to keep the family system alive and well.

Social coping. In the next level of coping, social coping, we seek support from others in our social network to help us deal with stress. Social support is one of the most widely studied constructs in the stress and coping research, and it is arguably one of the most important coping resources available to individuals and families (Gardner & Cutrona, 2004). In a review of the stress, coping, and social support literatures, Peggy Thoits (1995) classified social support as a coping resource – "a social 'fund' from which people may draw when handling stressors" (p. 64) – rather than a coping strategy. Researchers from this viewpoint examine either the direct effects of being a member of a social group (when higher levels of social integration are associated with better health) or the indirect effects on stress (when they buffer the individual from the negative impacts of stress)

(Burleson & MacGeorge, 2002; Thoits, 1995). Other scholars, such as Gardner and Cutrona (2004), focus on the actual supportive behaviors from the support-giver's point of view, defining social support as "verbal communication or behavior that is responsive to another's needs" (p. 495). This perspective is more closely aligned with a functional perspective that examines how social support can help us in times of need: for example, by offering comfort (emotional support), reassurance of worth (esteem support), expressions of connection (network support), information and advice (informational support), tangible assistance, or new perspectives (appraisal support) (Burleson & MacGeorge, 2002). Either way, the strategy of support-seeking is one of the most common forms of coping, and is present in nearly every comprehensive system that attempts to document ways of coping (Skinner et al., 2002).

Communal coping. Although research on coping at the individual and social levels has been around for decades, a promising theoretical approach to understand coping from a family perspective is beginning to get attention: communal coping (Afifi, Hutchinson, & Krouse, 2006; Lyons et al., 1998). Communal coping happens when multiple individuals who are affected by the same stressor pool their resources and efforts in order to face adversity. As such, "communal coping is a process in which a stressful event is substantively appraised and acted upon in the context of close relationships" (Lyons et al., 1998, p. 583). In order for communal coping to occur, one or more of the members of the family must perceive the problem as "our" problem, as opposed to just "my" or "your" problem.

An important assumption behind communal coping is that the family members have the desire, resources, and skills to come together to face stress. When they do, communal coping expands the family's resources and capacity to deal with stress, because it represents an investment in the relationship, and, of course, buffers stress (Lyons et al., 1998). Yet, communal coping may not be the best strategy for a family. For example, some stressors may be more individually oriented in the first place and not deemed "our" problem; in such cases, communal coping may not be an effective way to manage these situations. In addition, communal coping may be more appropriate in cultures that take a communitarian approach to solving problems (Lyons et al., 1998). Finally, communal coping may negatively impact families with discrepant views on the function of openness in relational communication. For instance, families that believe parents and children should discuss ideas openly are likely to share ideas, participate in group decision making, and express concerns; thus, they may be more likely to use communal coping strategies than families low on this orientation, in which members interact less frequently with one another on a variety of topics (Koerner & Fitzpatrick, 1997).

In order to help students and scholars of family interaction differentiate communal coping from other types of coping, Afifi et al. (2006) proposed a theoretical model that attempts to capture the "interdependent and transactional nature of the coping process" within the family system (p. 382) (see Figure 3.1). According to the model, coping efforts differ according to our appraisals of stressor ownership ("my/your/our" stress) and responsibility for coping ("my/your/our" responsibility). One form of coping mirrors the traditional view of stress and coping enacted at the individual level to manage one's own distress ("my problem, my responsibility"). From the scenario at the start of the chapter, for instance, Christine may see the stress related to writing her research paper as her own issue that she needs to cope with on her own (that is, deal with the problem by doing the work). Another form of coping happens when a family member appraises a stressor as "our problem, my responsibility:" we are facing the same stressor, but it is *my* responsibility to cope with the problem. Christine, her mother, and her sister each feel that the father's heart disease is a family problem, and thus each one enacts strategies to support the father in parallel with each other (but not together as a group – that would be communal coping). Christine, on the other hand, may feel she is helping her family by not telling them about the other stressors in her life, a strategy called protective buffering, defined by Afifi et al. (2006) as the shielding of another family member or the group as a whole from a stressor.

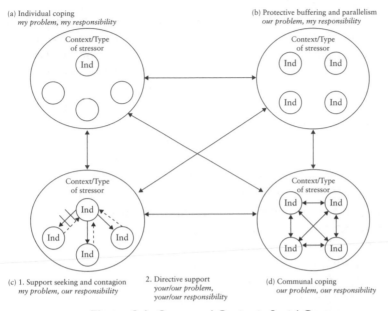

Figure 3.1: Communal Coping in Social Groups.
Reproduced with permission of John Wiley and Sons

In the model, *social coping* ("my problem, our responsibility") occurs when a family member either directly asks others for help with a problem or "indirectly" asks for help when his or her stress "spills over" onto other family members (emotional contagion). Whereas Christine's mother is more likely to specifically ask for support from her daughters, Christine's sister may be more apt to cry or complain until someone helps her. An additional form of social coping, *directive coping* (asking other family members to assume responsibility for a stressor), happens when a family member appraises a stressor as "your/our problem, your/our responsibility" but believes that other members do not see it the same way; thus, they tell the others what to do to cope. Christine may feel that the inability for her and her partner to discuss their future is a joint problem and should be acted upon together; yet, Christine feels frustrated when her partner does not join in on these conversations, thus, she tells her partner how she feels and what needs to change. Finally, *communal coping* happens when family members "assume mutual responsibility for a stressor and act on it together in a proactive manner" (p. 381). For this type of coping to occur, family members must appraise the stress as "our stress, our responsibility," as when Christine, her mother, and her sister all work together to create a new family mealtime routine for the father.

Throughout the preceding discussion, coping was considered in the context of a stressor that already happened in the past or is unfolding in the present. Grounded in the positive psychology movement where researchers are searching for ways to build the positive qualities in people (vs repairing the worst things in life) (Seligman & Csikszentmihalyi, 2000), some scholars include future-oriented coping strategies in their research. These strategies are used in advance of a potential stressor (such as a potential lay-off) in order to prevent or mute the negative impact of the event (Folkman & Moskowitz, 2004).

Coping Outcomes

Despite the general similarities in the individual and family approaches to the study of coping, there is one place where the two literatures seem to diverge. Whereas scholars from the individual perspective, particularly those who follow the work of Lazarus, insist on separating coping strategies from coping outcomes, family scholars do not seem as adamant in this separation, despite what their models depict. Instead, family scholars tend to equate family coping with success. Boss (2002) states that "coping is more than a resource; it is also an outcome variable, meaning that the family is coping (managing) and thus is not in crisis" (p. 89). In this way, Boss talks of "functional coping" and researchers' quest to understand how families adapt to stressful situations to avoid crisis, or how they emerge from a crisis situation to become as functional, if not more so, as they were before the crises – the focus of the family resilience research. The next section discusses both issues in more depth.

Coping as Separate from Outcomes vs Coping as Adaptation

Recall that one of the principal tenets of the process approach to coping is to avoid labeling a coping strategy as "adaptive" or "maladaptive" from the start. Lazarus and Folkman (1984) assert that the "goodness (efficacy, appropriateness) of a strategy is determined only by its effects in a given encounter and its effects in the long term" (p. 134). From this perspective, coping strategies and coping outcomes are two separate variables, each of which needs to be interpreted within a given context. That is not to say that coping outcomes do not matter. Indeed, Lazarus and Folkman identify both short-term and long-term adaptation outcomes of the coping process along three levels: (a) social functioning (the immediate effects of coping efforts on regulating distress and managing the problem vs the long-term, repeated use of specific patterns of coping), (b) morale (feelings about how the coping process went in specific events vs tendencies to effectively manage a wide range of demands), and (c) somatic health and illness (increased neurochemical responses vs long-term health effects). Instead, what Lazarus and colleagues are saying is that some strategies that may appear "maladaptive" at a surface level, such as denial of a stressor or social withdrawal, may actually be effective in the short term, because they allow us to manage our immediate emotional reaction to a stressor. Similarly, it is just as problematic to say that active, confrontive coping strategies are always the best course of action, particularly in situations that are out of our control. In these instances, repeated attempts to change or address an irresolvable problem may result in increased feelings of frustration and distress, as opposed to decreased stress or improved mood. Even something as positive as affectionate communication could be seen in a negative light, particularly if it is perceived as disingenuous or if it is not reciprocated (Floyd & Pauley, 2011). As Spitzberg (1994) warns that, "Virtually any behavior, when used in the extreme, is likely to be incompetent" (p. 38).

Research on family stress, on the other hand, tends to focus on the extent to which families employ a host of adaptive or functional coping responses, often leaving out or denigrating the more "negative" strategies. Burr et al. (1994), for instance, created a typology of family coping strategies based on a review of the research, resulting in a final set of seven coping "families": (a) cognitive, (b) emotional, (c) relationships, (d) communication, (e) community, (f) spiritual, and (g) individual development. While Burr et al. also mentioned strategies aimed at avoiding or resolving disabling expressions of emotion – such as passivity or spending time together without talking about stressors or other issues – they specifically labeled such strategies "maladaptive," saying, "These are not considered effective ways to resolve concerns about the specific situation; in fact, the behaviors enable family members to avoid expressing emotion" (p. 141). Yet, communication research has found that ambiguity may be useful when the nature of the problem is not completely understood (e.g., Beach, 2001); avoidance can help protect privacy boundaries and is not necessarily detrimental to relationships (e.g., Caughlin & Afifi, 2004); and too much cohesion can prevent individual family members from speaking out for fear they will "rock the boat" and damage the family relationship (e.g., Afifi & Olson, 2005). Burr et al. also claim that although scholars have cited harmful or disabling coping responses such as violence, or alcohol or drug use, they chose to leave such responses out of their typology because they were few in number and considered ineffective in stress management.

There are a number of possible reasons why some family stress scholars tend to associate family coping with positive outcomes. First, they could be reacting to the early studies of stress in families that sought "to document the psychological, interpersonal, and social aberrations in the family's response to stressors and related hardships" (McCubbin et al., 1980). Researchers from the more "modern" approach to coping research, likely the result of the positive psychology movement, have attempted to discover why some families are better able to handle hardships than others; they view stress as a normal, and not necessarily problematic, aspect of family life. Second, perhaps the less prosocial, more aggressive forms of coping may be relegated to the individual level, where family members cope with their own immediate emotional reactions to a stressor by lashing out, isolating themselves from the rest of the family, or building smaller coalitions within the family to get support for their point of view. In support of this assumption, Menaghan (1983) created a taxonomy of coping efforts, based on focus of action, where she identified a number of strategies that could be employed at both the individual and family level. Whereas all of the pro-social, problem-focused strategies occurred at both levels, two emotion-focused strategies (expression/release and suppression/restraint) occurred only at the individual level. She did provide examples at both levels for another emotion-management strategy: diversion. Once again, these examples were pro-social (such as joint participation in cohesive building activities or shared rituals), emphasizing the positive nature of coping processes in the study of family stress.

Third, some of the strategies identified in the research as negative lie at the extreme end of "bad news" ways of coping (Skinner et al., 2002) – violence, or drug or alcohol use, for example. There is little argument that these coping responses are destructive at both the individual and family levels. Then again, some family scholars automatically classify as problematic other, less hostile actions families may employ to cope with emotional reactions to stress. Burr et al. (1994), for example, categorized the communication strategy "keep others from knowing how bad the situation is" as harmful in their study of family stress and coping across various contexts. Although a majority of respondents in their studies agreed that the strategy was not helpful, some participants did rate this form of protective buffering as helpful, particularly when coping with stressors such as bankruptcy or illness.

Regardless of the reason, family scholars should be wary of labeling certain strategies as adaptive or maladaptive without considering their context. For instance, Leslie Baxter, a communication scholar, finds it problematic that many researchers tend to evaluate "closeness" as positive and "distance" as negative and symptomatic of a problem. She claims that we must understand both processes in order to gain a complete picture of family life.

Instead of silencing oppositional forces in family life by leaving them out of coping typologies, researchers from a dialectical view would posit that they should be included in studies of stress, because, as Baxter (2006) observes, "Contradictory voices permeate communication, and it is their interplay that constructs meaning for family members" (p. 132).

Research that focuses on just the positive coping strategies also fails to recognize that even those positive strategies may sometimes become problematic. Because of the interdependent nature of family life, individual, social, or communal coping efforts can result in unexpected, often negative, consequences (Afifi et al., 2006; Maguire & Sahlstein, 2009). Indeed, Afifi et al. (2006) propose, "family members' stress and coping abilities are interdependent with the stress and coping abilities of other family members (i.e., one person's stress and coping affects the others)" (p. 403), suggesting that different coping efforts can interfere with one another and cause further problems. These "coping paradoxes" (when helpful coping efforts exacerbate rather than mitigate the effects of stress; Dolan & Ender, 2008) are likely to occur in a number of circumstances, as when one partner's stress starts to affect the other (Bodenmann, 2005), when one family member's choice of coping response causes distress in other family members (Wethington & Kessler, 1991), or when family members have discrepant views about the role of communication in the coping process (Hilton & Koop, 1994). At the same time, it is important to identify the coping responses associated with adaptive outcomes in the research so as to pinpoint sources of strength that help families survive or thrive during difficult times (Seligman & Csikszentmihalyi, 2000). Family researchers interested in family resilience often try to determine what differentiates successful families from those that have more difficulty coping with crisis.

Family Resilience

Stemming from this preference for the positive, Boss (2002) equates functional coping with resilience, one of the most commonly studied outcomes in the family stress research. Froma Walsh, a leading researcher in family resilience, defines *resilience* as "the ability to withstand and rebound from disruptive life challenges"; she sees it as a critical process that "fosters the ability to 'struggle well,' heal from painful experiences, and go on to live and love fully" (Walsh, 2003, p. 399).

Richardson (2002) tracked the evolution of the study of resilience at the individual level which can be used to understand resilience at the family level as well. In the first wave, researchers sought to understand why some children could thrive in the face of extreme adversity while others faltered (see Werner & Smith, 1992). This approach signaled a fundamental shift from a focus on factors that place us at risk of harm to protective factors (such as optimism, self-determination, faith, wisdom, creativity) that nurture personal strengths and help us recover from adversity. The second wave in the study of resilience focused on understanding how we acquire resilient qualities, and viewed resilience as a "process of coping with stressors, adversity, change, or opportunity in a manner that results in the identification, fortification, and enrichment of protective factors" (Richardson, 2002, p. 308). From this view, the term *resilience* was expanded to include not only recovering or bouncing back from adversity, but also growth. The third wave, which Richardson characterizes as postmodern and interdisciplinary, seeks to go beyond merely identifying protective factors and understanding the process through which we acquire resilience to a more esoteric, theoretical level that embraces disciplines ranging from physics and biology to psychology, theology, and mysticism. According to Richardson (2002), "there is a force within everyone that drives them to seek self-actualization, altruism, wisdom, and harmony with a spiritual source of strength. This force is resilience . . .," a characteristic that emerges from our ecosystem (p. 313).

Research in the family literature parallels Richardson's three waves of resilience research, although not necessarily in chronological order. For instance, Black and Lobo (2008) identified a number of protective and recovery factors prominent among resilient families (thus paralleling the first wave of resilience research), including (a) a positive, optimistic outlook on life; (b) spirituality; (c) family member accord and cohesion; (d) flexibility (the ability to make structural or situational adjustments in family roles as needed); (e) family communication (characterized by clarity and collaborative problem solving); (f) financial management; (g) family time; (h) shared recreation; (i) routines and rituals to promote close family relationships even during times of crisis; and (j) individual, family, and community support networks. In studies of family resilience as a process (the second wave), researchers often include the concept of risk because it signifies that dysfunctional behavior and reduced family functioning are possible outcomes of the situation (Patterson, 2002). It is here that a family crisis could occur: Families at risk often have a persistent imbalance between the demands they face and their capabilities (resources and coping), which creates a period of disequilibrium and disorganization in family life. This period of chaos is also a turning point at which the family may enact significant changes to emerge from the crisis. A resilient family, then, is one that makes the necessary changes to emerge from crisis as a stronger, more resourceful family than before the ordeal (Walsh, 2003). McCubbin and Patterson (1983) labeled family reintegration in this post-crisis period "bonadaptation."

In regard to the third wave, although some researchers see resilience as an innate quality of a family (that is, a family either is or is not resilient), many family scholars believe every family is capable of becoming resilient. Recall that Boss (2002) suggests a family may need to fall into crisis in order to radically change a system of interaction that continues to harm individuals in the family or the family as a whole. It is through this process that the family acquires protective factors to help it in future crises. Family scholars also agree that resilience emerges from and is related to our ecosystem or contextual environment. Walsh (2003), for example, believes that the family, the support network, community resources, school or work, and other social settings interact to facilitate and nurture resilience. Likewise, Boss (2002) includes external contextual factors such as culture, economy, heredity, and history in her Contextual Model of Family Stress.

Summary

As you can see from this chapter, coping is a complex, multi-faceted process that takes many forms and performs several functions. Scholars at the individual level have focused on the ways we manage stress to avoid any negative consequences resulting from our encounters with stressors. At the family level, researchers have focused on what families can do to help ensure they successfully adjust to stress or adapt after a crisis. Although both the individual and family perspectives place meaning-making activities (cognitive appraisals in the individual perspective, meaning and perceptions at the family level) at the forefront, and emphasize the role that values, beliefs, expectations, and motivations have in the meaning-making process, they diverge in two ways. First, whereas the individual approach to coping differentiates coping strategies from coping outcomes, the family approach appears to equate coping with effectiveness and adaptation, essentially confounding the two processes. Second, whereas the individual approach to coping includes the involvement of other people in the form of social support, the family approach to coping recognizes that family members and loved ones play a larger role in the coping process, both as targets for coping efforts (relationship maintenance) and as co-participants in the coping process (communal coping). It is here that we begin to see the various ways communication affects the coping process. Chapter 4 explores these connections by reviewing scholarship from communication and relational researchers who focus on the messages family members exchange during the stress and coping processes, and how these messages affect, and are affected by, stress.

4

Communication within the Stress and Coping Processes

It is 11:00 a.m., and Christine feels like she has been up for hours – not because of working late, but because of the conversation she just had with her partner. Over a nice breakfast, she brought up her concerns about renting a house together, because it implies both a financial and legal commitment that Christine wonders if she is ready to make. The conversation went in a different direction than Christine anticipated when her partner talked about a mutual friend who just moved into a beautiful condo with his significant other. It left Christine frustrated and a bit confused as to why her partner is so reluctant to talk about her concerns. Toward the end of the meal, Christine confronted her partner about being evasive, only to find herself staring in shock as her partner walked out of the room, saying, "Can you just leave it alone? We'll talk about it soon, okay?" Conversations like this make Christine wonder whether she and her partner are compatible after all. On the one hand, Christine likes to confront problems, which often means talking about the problem so she can see all sides of the situation before taking action. On the other hand, Christine's partner likes to spend time alone, thinking about the problem before talking about it. If Christine talks before her partner is ready, they both end up stressed. For now, all Christine can do is hope that things will change as they both adjust to each other and create new ways of communicating that overcome such obstacles.

At the start of every chapter thus far, you have been reading a "case study" that illustrates how close relational partners and family members can be our greatest resource or our biggest obstacle as we cope with stress. Within each scenario, you can also see how communication functions in the coping process. In some instances, communication is an important coping resource and strategy that allows families to find meaning in a stressor, alleviate feelings of distress, connect with loved ones, or manage problems. The way Christine's family is handling her father's heart disease, for instance, is a good example of how families can work together in times of stress. In other instances, such as Christine's ill-fated discussions with her partner about their future, communication becomes a source of stress or an indication that something is wrong in the family system.

Although researchers from disciplines such as family sociology and psychology also talk about the importance of communication in the stress and coping processes, they do so in a limited way. For example, psychologists discuss communication in the context of social support, where communication is implied, but not directly studied, as the way we seek help from others in times of need. Communication scholars, however, view social support (as well as other forms of coping) as a dynamic process influenced by the messages family members simultaneously send and receive in times of stress – a process that sometimes results in unhelpful support (Gardner & Cutrona, 2004). In addition, family sociologists suggest that openness and family cohesion are best practices for families under stress (e.g., Black & Lobo, 2008). Instead of claiming that one type of coping approach (such as open communication) is better than other, seemingly unproductive forms of communication (such as venting or withdrawing), the approach in this book recognizes that coping efforts have varying, sometimes unexpected, effects on family members (Afifi et al., 2006; Maguire & Sahlstein, 2009).

In this fourth chapter, you will read about communication in the coping process. The chapter begins with a definition of communication that captures the complexity of communication in the family context. Next, you will encounter a communication-based model of the coping process that will structure the remainder of the chapter, which outlines the various roles and functions of communication in the coping process: communication as stressor and/or symptom, as meaning-making, as resource, as a coping strategy, and as an outcome of the coping process.

Defining Communication

Following the example of family communication scholars such as Galvin and colleagues (Galvin et al., 2008) and Turner and West (2006), *communication* is broadly defined as a symbolic process through which meaning is made. Defining communication in this way goes beyond simplistic interactional definitions of communication to include the meaning-making process. For example, in the book *Clinical Manual for Couples and Family Therapy*, the authors define *communication* as "the exchange of information within a family" (Keitner, Heru, & Glick, 2010, p. 16). Such an exchange-based model of communication, situated within the family systems perspective, emphasizes how the act of communication binds people together, an dates back to the early work of Burgess (1926) and later to the seminal work, *The Pragmatics of Human Communication* by Watzlawick, Bavelas, and Jackson (1967). Whereas information exchange is an important component of the communication process within families, conceptualizing communication as an exchange of information via interaction paints a picture of communication as static, straightforward, and easily accomplished. A deeper look at the primary components of the definition used in this book reveals that communication is a dynamic, complex, and fluid process that changes over time and across relationships.

First, the term *symbolic* denotes that the meaning associated with verbal and nonverbal messages used to create, negotiate, or negate meaning is somewhat arbitrary, in that different people can have different meanings for the same word, phrase, or action. For example, family members often say "I love you" to one another. For some, this phrase indicates that they have an abiding affection for one another; others say it because they are committed to making the relationship work (without the accompanying message of affection) or because it is a formality with no real meaning behind it. The adage, "meaning is in people, not words" applies to this situation. A diversity of meanings can lead to problems if the family members do not share a common "code" or way of speaking to communicate a particular meaning. During times of stress, it may be particularly easy to misinterpret what someone else says, leading family members to act on what they perceive to be reality instead of checking to make sure that their interpretation is "accurate."

The term *process* is also important, because it implies that communication is always changing. At one moment, the words "I love you" can carry great weight and help alleviate our stress; at another moment, the words fall on deaf ears because we doubt the sincerity of the message or need something more to help us cope with stress. Because they view communication as a process, communication scholars recognize the difficulty in saying that certain messages or approaches to communication are problematic or always preferred over other forms of communication (for example, that openness is always good, or that deception is always bad).

Finally, the focus on *meaning-making* suggests that our understandings about things, events, and relationships (their meaning) emerge through our interactions with others. From this perspective, families create their own social world, in which meaning emerges as family members "interact with each other; as they share time, space, and life experiences; and as they talk with each other and dialogue about these experiences" (Patterson & Garwick, 1994, p. 288). Families use these meaning systems to appraise stressful situations and to guide their actions as they cope with stress.

A Communication-Based Coping Model

With the definition of communication outlined above in mind, I offer the following communication-based model of the coping process which identifies the varying roles that communication

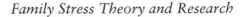

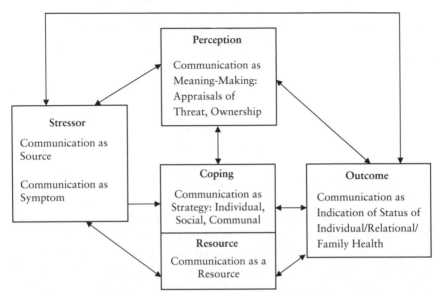

Figure 4.1: A Communication-Based Model of Coping in the Family System

plays throughout the process in order to better understand the full range of family communication during times of stress (see Figure 4.1). I derived the primary components of the model from the models discussed in Chapters 2 and 3, and included multiple double-headed arrows to indicate that the stressor, resource, perception, coping, and outcome factors all interact with one another as families face stressful situations. The difference in this model from the others lies in its focus on communication within each of the five major factors: (a) communication as a source or symptom of stress; (b) communication as meaning-making; (c) communication as strategy; (d) communication as resource; and (e) communication as an indication of the status of individual, relational, or family health. Whereas some of these functions have received a great deal of attention in communication scholarship (communication as stress, meaning-making, resource, strategy), others have received less attention (communication as a symptom meaning-making or an indication of functioning). Where there is a vast body of research, I highlight the programs of research that most clearly demonstrate how family and relational communication scholars contribute to the research on family stress and coping. Where there is more limited research, I discuss communication scholarship that applies to that particular function, proposing connections that could guide future research. Although communication studies have often escaped the notice of family scholars from disciplines like sociology, psychology, and counseling, they offer a clear contribution to the research that expands our understanding of how messages affect, and are affected by, stress and coping in the family system.

Communication as a Source or Symptom of Stress

First, a great deal of communication scholarship considers some types of communication as a source of stress, particularly when communication or relational needs are not being met within the family system, when the relationships within the family are troubled, or when the messages or the interactions are stress-provoking. Tamara Afifi, one of the leading communication scholars in family stress and coping research, has studied stressful situations such as "feeling caught" in stepfamilies (Afifi & Schrodt, 2003), ambiguous loss in post-divorce stepfamilies (Afifi & Keith, 2004), and stressful or inappropriate disclosures within military marriages (Joseph & Afifi, 2010) and civilian families (Afifi, McManus, Hutchinson, & Baker, 2007). The model of communal coping in social groups discussed in Chapter 3 that she helped to develop highlights the interdependent nature of family life and the critical role communication plays in the coping process (Afifi et al., 2006). Research on interpersonal conflict also emphasizes interdependence, suggesting that conflict, while a normal and unavoidable part of relational life, can be stressful (Floyd & Afifi, 2011; Reznik, Roloff, & Miller, 2010; Roloff & Chiles, 2011). Indeed, Sillars, Canary, and Tafoya (2004) state that conflict is one of the most studied subjects in family communication, because "conflict represents the side of family interaction that family members themselves find difficult, unsettling, and perplexing" (p. 413).

Communication scholarship within the broad category of the "dark side" of interpersonal communication (Spitzberg & Cupach, 1994; 2007) also provides examples of communication serving as sources of stress. As discussed in Chapter 1, hurtful messages, for instance, can be a significant source of stress (e.g., McLaren & Solomon, 2008; Priem, McLaren, & Solomon, 2010; Theiss, Knobloch, Checton, & Magsamen-Conrad, 2009; Vangelisti, 1994; Vangelisti et al., 2007; Young, Kubicka, Tucker, Chavez-Appel, & Rex, 2005). Priem et al. (2010) hypothesized that hurtful interactions between romantic partners would elicit a physiological stress response in the recipient because such messages potentially pose a threat to our self-identity and/or relational identity. They found that feelings of hurt were associated with short-term spikes in the stress hormone, cortisol. If romantic partners communicated these messages at the same time as messages of liking, however, then the recipient experienced less increase in stress over time and reported feeling less hurt. Thus, the *way* the message is communicated might predict how a recipient could respond (for example, with forgiveness, withdrawal, or lashing out). Other examples of stressful communication include social allergens (repeated behaviors enacted by one partner, like noisily belching or being rude, that result in feelings of disgust in the other partner; Cunningham, Shamblen, Barbee, & Ault, 2005), aggressive acts (Dailey, Lee, & Spitzberg, 2007), uncertainty (Colaner & Kranstuber, 2010; Knobloch, 2008; Maguire, 2007), abuse (Olson, 2004), teasing and bullying (Kowalski, 2007), deception (Knapp, 2008), family secrets (Afifi & Olson, 2005; Vangelisti, 1994), and relational transgressions (violations of relationship rules such as infidelity, breaking a significant promise, or violating a confidence; Metts, 1994).

Whereas communication can be a source of stress, it can also be a *symptom* of underlying stress in the family system. According to Boss (2002), when a family is in crisis, the focus shifts from the family to the individual as the system ceases functioning and family members become unable to care for one another as they once had. This shift in focus may lead to doubts about family members' commitment to one another, which can significantly influence communicative activity among family members (Solomon & Knobloch, 2004). For example, family members may distance themselves emotionally from one another to cope with their own feelings of distress (Repetti & Wood, 1997). Family members may also act out against one another, verbally or physically venting their frustrations and negative emotions (Langer, Lawrence, & Barry, 2008). In a study of aggression during the early years of marriage, Langer et al. (2008) found that 62% of the couples in their study (44% of husbands and 54% of wives) had been physically aggressive in their relationship. Although personality traits such as impulsivity and aggressiveness were associated with more physical aggression, increases in chronic stress also predicted increases in physical aggression. The authors explained that chronic stress demands more emotional resources, leaving couples less able to interact with one another in positive, pro-social, and adaptive ways. If family members do not have the skills to cope effectively with stress, they may turn to aggressive tactics under stressful conflict situations in an attempt to "resolve" the situation (Infante, Chandler, & Rudd, 1989; Segrin, 2001).

Research on common couple violence suggests that couples sometimes become aggressive during conflict episodes that get "out of hand," leading to "minor" (e.g., a shove) or even more serious forms of violence (a brutal attack) (Johnson, 1995, p. 285). Common couple violence differs from more systemic types of domestic violence, such as patriarchal terrorism, wherein husbands control their wives through physical violence, economic subordination, threats, isolation, and other control tactics. In a study of common couple violence during conflict episodes, Olson (2002) described some relationships as "aggressive relationships," wherein both members of the couple acted aggressively, often in a reciprocal fashion. Unlike abusive couples, whose relationships revealed a marked power imbalance, couples in aggressive relationships shared power and had generally healthy communication: They would talk about the aggressive episode and had low tolerance for aggression when it occurred.

Communication as Meaning-Making

Communication also plays an important role as families perceive a stressor and find meaning in stressful circumstances, which is the "C" factor in Hill's (1949) ABC-X Model of Family Crisis. According to Patterson and Garwick (1994), family members collectively construct meanings through interaction as they share life experiences and talk with one another about these experiences. A number of theoretical perspectives embrace the meaning-making function of communication, including Social Constructionism (Gergen & Davis, 1985), Symbolic Interactionism (Blumer, 1969), Narrative Theory (Fisher, 1987), Narrative Performance Theory (Langellier & Peterson, 2004), and the Coordinated Management of Meaning (Pearce & Cronen, 1980). All of these theories can be applied to how families make sense of stressful circumstances through the stories and narratives they create in the meaning-making process.

One way families create meaning is through storytelling (Boss, 2002). Bochner (2002) explains the importance of storytelling in our personal and relational lives, tying it directly to adaptation:

> Stories are the narrative frames within which we make our experiences meaningful . . . The success with which we cope with the contingencies of our interpersonal lives depends largely on how effectively we respond to the contradictions and conflicts that social life necessarily poses. The narratives we create, discover, and apply help us maintain a sense of coherence and continuity over the course of our lives.
>
> (pp. 73–74)

Fiese and Pratt (2004) also believe stories are important because they "serve the key role of constructing *meaning* and a sense of identity, both for the individual and the wider family" (p. 413, original emphasis retained). Similarly, Langellier and Peterson (2004) emphasize the ubiquitous nature of storytelling in family life, stating that "Families perform stories . . . they have something to say or to figure out how to say, stories old and new to tell, and habitual and innovative ways of working together to tell these stories" (p. 100).

A small but growing body of communication research examines family storytelling and its role in constructing not only family identity, but family meaning and individual health as well. Jody Koenig Kellas is at the forefront of research on family storytelling; her work looks at shared joint storytelling, or "the process by which family members construct stories in interaction . . . to help them make sense of and give meaning to the event(s) and to their relationships" (Koenig Kellas, 2005, p. 366). According to Koenig Kellas, family stories of stressful situations show not only how the family typically responds to stress, but also the extent to which the family has "let go" of the stressful experience or, instead, has woven it in as part of the fabric of the family's identity. In her study, she asked 60 family triads to recount a frequently told family story that describes what the family is like. Whereas most of the families told stories about accomplishment, fun, tradition/culture, separateness, togetherness, and child mischief, 13 families told stories that focused on stressful situations. These 13 families had significantly lower levels of satisfaction, family functioning, family cohesions, and family adaptability than those that told stories about accomplishment. She offers three explanations for why this may be the case: (a) families that are less satisfied, functional, cohesive, and adaptable are less able to find positive stories to explain themselves; (b) stressful experiences predominate in families that are less happy and/or functional; or (c) families that are less satisfied may have trouble framing stories in a positive way. In any case, these families define themselves by their stressful experiences and appear to find meaning in their *inability* to effectively handle difficult situations.

In addition to linking family storytelling with relational well-being, family storytelling is reflective of positive relational interactions and predictive of individual well-being. In one study of family storytelling, families that engaged in storytelling as a meaning-making activity were more engaged and attentive to one another than those that do not (Koenig Kellas & Trees, 2006). In regards to individual well-being, Koenig Kellas and colleagues (Koenig Kellas, Trees, Schrodt, LeClair-Underberg, & Willer, 2010) asserted that telling a story about a stressful experience "allows an individual to express emotions and/or cognitively make sense of the trauma, which in turn allows the individual to 'let go' of the memory and move on from potentially unhealthy ruminations" (p. 176). In their study of the stories marital couples jointly tell about their stressful experiences, the researchers found that when both spouses told an organized and integrated story dynamically, the husband exhibited fewer symptoms of mental health problems. When the stories had a good deal of narrative coherence, or when the wife took her husband's perspective, the husband reported lower levels of perceived stress. The reverse was true as well: the more the husband took his wife's perspective and was engaged with her throughout the storytelling process, the more mentally healthy he was.

Communication as a Resource

Another way that communication functions in the family stress process is as a coping resource. One of the most frequently studied resources is social support, viewed from a sociological perspective as a "social 'fund' from which people may draw when handling stressors" (Thoits, 1995, p. 64). In a review of the communication research regarding social support, Gardner and Cutrona (2004) conclude, "Support from family members is a valuable resource. Its presence can reduce stress and promote fulfillment and security. Its absence can magnify the damage sustained by adversity life conditions and limit the joy of intimacy with others" (p. 506). Whereas studies of enacted support – that is, studies of what people actually do or say – demonstrate that social support reduces the negative effects of stress on well-being, Goldsmith (2004) also notes that enacted support can have no effect, or even a negative effect, on well-being as well; examples of *unhelpful* forms of social support include criticism, unwanted advice, minimization of problems, and discomfort on the part of the support provider.

Family communication is also an important coping resource. Black and Lobo (2008) list clarity, openness, and collaborative problem solving as important factors in family resilience, asserting that "Harmonious communication is the essence of how families create a shared sense of meaning, develop coping strategies, and maintain agreement and balance" (p. 42). In particular, research on family communication patterns suggests that a family's ability to use communication as a resource during stressful times may depend on family members' internal working models, or *schemata*, of communication and relationships (Afifi & Olson, 2005; Fitzpatrick & Ritchie, 1994; Ritchie, 1991; Schrodt, Witt, & Messersmith, 2008). According to Schrodt et al. (2008), "schemata emerge from working models of how parents and children interact, and ultimately, shape how family members perceive their social environments and communicate within and outside of the family" (p. 249).

Ritchie (1991) identified two dimensions that describe family interaction: one characterized by supportive and open communication and the other characterized by conformity and control. A family high in *conversation* orientation is concerned with open discussion of ideas between parents and children: Everyone shares ideas, participates in decision making, and expresses concerns. A family high in *conformity* orientation, on the other hand, is concerned with homogeneity of attitudes, beliefs, and values among all family members, and tends to have hierarchical family structures that prioritize family interests above those of individual family members. In a study of the family communication patterns research, Schrodt et al. (2008) reported that conversation-orientation predicts outcomes such as improved physical/mental health, self-esteem, family cohesion, and relational satisfaction because it "equips children with the information processing skills and communication behaviors necessary for coping with stress and for developing healthy relationships outside of the family" (p. 263). In this regard, a family high in conversation orientation is likely to value communication as a resource when faced with a stressor. Afifi and Olson (2005) note that families high in conformity orientation and low in conversation orientation may pressure family members to conceal family secrets, resulting in lower feelings of closeness and commitment to one another. On the other hand, families high in conversation orientation may continuously disclose potentially conflict-inducing secrets until closeness begins to erode, at which point they may more carefully regulate what they reveal.

Consider two families: the Rodriguez family, a working class family from San Antonio, and the Young family, an inner-city family from Detroit. Both families are facing extreme economic hardship, as the primary breadwinner in each family was recently laid off from a job: Rick Rodriguez from a construction company that makes single-family homes, and Angela Young from an auto supply company that makes parts for luxury cars. When Rick first suspected he was going to be laid-off from his job, he called a family meeting so that he, his partner, and their two teenage daughters could brainstorm ways to earn and save money. As a group, they decided to cancel their cable and internet services and eat all their meals at home. His partner, Josh, offered to trade in his SUV for a more fuel-efficient car, and decided to sell his motorcycle to start a savings account. The girls said they could start babysitting or find other part-time work to buy their own school supplies, clothes, and necessities. Because of their orientation toward shared decision making and sacrifice, they had the communication resources they needed to weather the reduction in economic resources until Rick got a new job.

Angela's family, on the other hand, had a more difficult time coping with the layoff. Like the Rodriguez family, they, too, got together as a group to talk about the situation, but only after it happened. Then, instead of coming to consensus and brainstorming solutions, Angela's husband, Stefan, dictated what everyone should do: Angela should apply for unemployment, look for a new job, and stop shopping; Bobbie and Sheila should give the money they earn watching their cousins every week so he could pay bills; and he would ask his parents for money to keep up his monthly car payment on his Mustang. No one questioned Stefan's decisions, although no one was happy with his choices; as a result, they withdrew further from the family. Whereas they were lucky to have the support of nearby family to help them out, they lacked sufficient family communication resources to help them come to a mutually satisfying solution.

Communication as a Coping Strategy

Coping strategies are often enacted via communication, which explains why a large body of communication research examines communicative coping strategies. Much of the coping research from family and relational communication scholars has investigated coping in very specific contexts, including infertility (Bute & Vik, 2010), post-divorce families (Afifi et al., 2006), grieving (Bosticco & Thompson, 2005), jealousy (Aune & Comstock, 2002), military deployment (Maguire & Sahlstein, in press), breast cancer (Donovan-Kicken & Caughlin, 2010; Fisher, 2010), and family-to-work spillover (Krouse & Afifi, 2007). Researchers have also studied particular forms of communication that can be used as coping strategies, such as topic avoidance (Donovan-Kicken & Caughlin, 2010), journaling (Caplan, Haslett, & Burleson, 2005), information-seeking (Hummelinck & Pollock, 2006), protective buffering (Joseph & Afifi, 2010), affectionate expression (Floyd, 2006), cooperation and joint problem-solving (Maguire & Kinney, 2010), uncertainty management (Brashers, 2001), relationship maintenance (Merolla, 2010), humor (Wanzer, Sparks, & Frymier, 2009), communal coping (Afifi et al., 2006), disclosure (Lewis & Manusov, 2009), and of course social support (Fisher, 2010).

For example, experimental work by Kory Floyd and his associates has shown that expressing affection to a close relational partner during a stressful episode, either verbally or in writing, has a moderating effect on physiological stress (Floyd & Afifi, 2011). Floyd et al. (2007) subjected 30 participants to various laboratory stressors (such as doing mental arithmetic or viewing marital conflict videos) to determine the effectiveness of affectionate expression in reducing acute stress symptoms (such as salivary cortisol level). They found that expressing love and affection in a letter to a loved one accelerates recovery from stress to a greater extent than just thinking about the loved one or sitting quietly. Thus, by saying "I love you" to family members, you not only ease their stress through such supportive messages, but also your own as well. A number of other researchers are attempting to link additional communication processes like social support, touch, communication competence, and responsiveness to physiological measures of stress and arousal in the body (salivary cortisol, alpha-amylase; see Floyd & Afifi, 2011, for a review).

Likewise, a small but growing body of communication research investigates how the strategies we use to sustain our relationships at a satisfactory level (relationship maintenance) can also be used in the coping process (Canary, Stafford, & Semic, 2002; Maguire & Kinney, 2010; Merolla, 2010). Communication strategies such as positivity (keeping the relationship upbeat and cheerful), assurances (committing to the continuance of the relationship), and openness (discussing the state of the relationship) are all examples of maintenance-focused coping responses, where partners engage in pro-social communication during stressful times in order to strengthen the relational bond (Maguire & Kinney, 2010). Strategies that fall under maintenance-focused coping have been identified in the family stress literature, dating back to the work of Hill (1949) and his focus on family integration as an important characteristic of families that adapted to wartime separation, as well as McCubbin (1979) and his inclusion of maintaining family integrity as a coping mechanism for families affected by wartime and work-related separation. Burr et al. (1994) cited several other examples of maintenance-focused coping enacted by families as well, including developing family cohesion and togetherness, building and improving trusting relationships with family members, and expressing feelings of affection for one another.

Some communication coping strategies can have negative, often unintended consequences. These coping paradoxes are common in interdependent groups like families (Afifi & McManus, 2010; Maguire & Sahlstein, 2011). For instance, families affected by a wartime deployment cope with the upcoming departure of their loved one by becoming emotionally distant from the person during a time when relational bonding is more important than ever (Maguire & Sahlstein, in press; Sahlstein et al., 2009). In another example, military wives tend to withhold disclosures about their stress from their deployed husbands when they perceive them to be in a dangerous location; however, such protective buffering is often associated with worse, not better, mental and health outcomes for wives (Joseph & Afifi, 2010). Likewise, in a study of communal coping in post-divorce families, some children reported that one parent would enlist their help in dealing with difficult relationships with the other parent, which left the children feeling "caught" in the middle (Afifi & McManus, 2010). Finally, despite the popular belief that venting negative emotions such as anger helps alleviate stress, research has revealed that communicative acts such as venting and catharsis actually serve to *increase* negative feelings and acts of violence (Lohr, Olatunji, Baumeister, & Bushman, 2007), which explains why this coping strategy is considered maladaptive in social relationships. A study by Harburg and colleagues (Harburg, Kaciroti, Gleiberman, Julius, & Schork, 2008), however, suggests that it is the *suppression* of anger in conflict, not the expression of anger, that may be associated with negative, long-term health outcomes in marriage, such as higher mortality.

Another paradox arises when family members' coping responses are at odds with each other. For example, in a study of spousal communication patterns in the context of breast cancer, Hilton and Koop (1994) found five different coping patterns, depending on the spouses' level of comfort with sharing and receiving emotional and cognitive information: (a) talkers, when both partners valued open communication in relationships; (b) moderate talkers, when both partners saw some value in open communication but in a limited way; (c) nontalkers, when both partners valued closed rather than open communication; (d) minorly discrepant couples, when the partners differed slightly in their value placed on open communication; and (e) majorly discrepant couples, when the partners disagreed greatly in their opinions about spousal communication. In their study, the single biggest factor determining a couple's adjustment to stress and their perceived satisfaction with the relationship was the degree of similarity in their opinions of open communication: discrepant couples were less satisfied and less adjusted than nondiscrepant couples. In short, whereas communication was useful for the couples with congruent perspectives on the value of talk in relationships, it was actually problematic for those couples with discrepant perspectives.

Likewise, the demand/withdrawal pattern that characterizes conflict in some family interactions, where demand implies an approach behavior (a desire to change the partner) and withdrawal implies an avoidance behavior (a desire to maintain the status quo), suggests that coping patterns may develop over time where one person wants to confront a problem and another wants to avoid. This may be the case with Christine and her partner, given her frustration with her partner's withdrawal every time she wants to talk about their future. If this pattern continues, Christine has good reason to be concerned about her relationship's future: the demand/withdrawal pattern has been associated with a number of negative outcomes, including increased distress (Malis & Roloff, 2006), marital dissatisfaction (Caughlin & Huston, 2002), and child unhappiness in post-divorce situations (Afifi & Schrodt, 2003). The demand/withdrawal pattern could also be a symptom of family dysfunction, and thus, an indication that the family is not adjusting or adapting well to stress. This may be the case when a family who once resolved conflict together starts to utilize oftentimes incompatible coping responses that could lead to additional distress.

As is evident from this brief review, as well as information from Chapter 3, scholars inside and outside the communication field have identified a large number of coping strategies. Following the example of researchers such as Skinner et al. (2002) and Burr et al. (1994) who created comprehensive coping typologies based on underlying features of coping, I offer a communication-based typology that accounts for the full range of coping responses in the family system and includes communication throughout the coping process to help make sense of this large body of literature (see Table 4.1). Communication is present throughout the typology, as both individuals and families use communication to seek assistance from others; confront or avoid problems; process and express thoughts, feelings, and ideas; manage interactions and maintain relationships; and create meaning. When combined, the matrix offers 35 different types of coping responses, ranging from individual-level, problem-focused behaviors such as researching the stressful situation (for example, reading about breast

Table 4.1. Organizational Schema to Understand Coping According to its Form, Function, and Level.

		Problem-Focused	Emotion-Focused	Meaning-Focused	Relationship-Focused	Maintenance-Focused
Behavior	*Individual*	Do research[4]	Drink[1]	Journal[2]	Shoulder responsibility[10]	Be physically affectionate[6]
	Social	Seek informational support[4]	Seek comfort[1]	Seek appraisal support[7]	Active engagement[8]	Seek network support[3]
	Communal	Family problem solving[6]	Group sharing of feelings[4]	Family storytelling[12]	Alterations in household management[5]	Cohesion-enhancing activities[4]
Cognition	*Individual*	Think through the problem[1]	Minimize distress[1]	Positive self-talk[1]	Take a family member's perspective[9]	Wear a symbol of the relationship (e.g., a ring)[2]
	Social	Seek strategizing support[11]	Seek counseling[6]	Pray[1]	Show empathy[9]	Talk about the family to others[2]
	Communal	Structure family life[5]	Reminisce about past successes[3]	Change definition of stressor[7]	Negotiate family rules[5]	Keep the memory of missing family member alive[3]
Avoidance	*Individual*	Self development[3]	Distraction[1]	Wishful thinking[1]	Conflict avoidance[6]	Distancing[1]
	Social	Give support outside the family[6]	Seek socializing support[6]	Blame others[1]	Protective buffering[8]	Develop relationships outside of the family[3]
	Communal	Reduce involvement[5]	Activities to ignore distress[1]	Family denial[3]	Family secrets[13]	Spend family time away from stressor[6]

Source: 1 = Skinner et al. (2002); 2 = Merolla, 2010; 3 = Boss (2002); 4 = Burr et al. (1994); 5 = Stetz et al. (1986); 6 = Maguire & Sahlstein (in press); 7 = Burleson & MacGeorge (2002); 8 = Coyne & Fiske (1992); 9 = DeLongis & O'Brien (1990); 10 = Hilton et al. (2000); 11 = Hobfoll et al. (1994); 12 = Koenig Kellas et al. (2010); 13 = Lyons et al. (1996).

cancer on the American Cancer Association's website) to social, meaning-focused cognitions such as prayer (seeking understanding from a higher power), to communal-level, maintenance-focused avoidance behaviors such as spending time as a family without worrying or thinking about the stressor (for example, family bowling night). You will see the matrix again in Chapters 5, 6, and 7 when you read about family stress and coping in very specific contexts.

Within this matrix, coping takes three primary forms (behavioral, cognitive, and avoidant), can fulfill five functions (problem-focused, emotion-focused, meaning-focused, relationship-focused, and maintenance-focused), and can occur along three levels (individual, social, and communal). First, as discussed in Chapter 3, there are three forms of coping. Behavioral responses occur when some concrete action is taken to cope with the situation. In a cognitive response, the action taken is more intangible because it happens in the individual or collective thought processes of family members. In responses that involve some sort of avoidance, individuals or family members keep away from or escape the stressful situation. Although avoidance responses can be cognitive or behavioral as well (for instance, distracting oneself by reading, or engaging in denial of a stressor), I am employing the division by Billings and Moos (1981), which classifies those behaviors or cognitions that are oriented *toward* the threat as approach responses versus those behaviors or cognitions that are oriented *away* from the threat as avoidance responses.

Second, in addition to the four coping functions discussed in Chapter 3 (to resolve, alter, or reduce the problem; to manage emotional reactions or distress; to create, change, or re-examine the meaning or appraisal of a stressor; to regulate interactions and meet one another's needs within the family relationship), I include a fifth coping function that emerged from the communication literature where strategies are enacted to maintain or strengthen relational bonds. Although there are five functions listed, it should be noted that the same strategy can serve multiple functions. For example, a family might work together to solve a problem and, in doing so, strengthen their relational bonds. In this example, the strategy is primarily problem-focused, but it also serves a secondary purpose: to maintain the relationship.

Third, coping occurs at a solitary, social, and/or communal level. I include individual coping, following the example of Boss (2002) who asserts that we need to understand all levels of coping to fully understand the family stress process. The inclusion of individual coping is also important as a family member's individual coping effort is likely to affect other family members, given the interdependent nature of family life. Whereas social coping involves seeking support from or giving support to individuals *outside* of the immediate family, communal coping involves working together as *a family unit* to enact the coping response. The exception to this pattern is the use of social strategies that fulfill a relationship-focused function, because these strategies are enacted within the family as they attempt to manage family interaction or meet family members' needs (for example, actively engaging one another in the coping process, employing empathic coping to gain understanding of other family members, or buffering family members from potentially bad news to protect them).

Communication as an Indication of the Status of Family Health and Functioning

The way a family communicates can also be an important indicator of family health and functioning, serving as a measure of both short-term and long-term outcomes of the coping process. In the case of maladaptation, where family functioning is lower than before the stressor occurred (McCubbin & Patterson, 1983), further withdrawal from the family, or when family members act aggressively toward one another, can be symptoms of unresolved problems in the family, particularly if an individual family member was hurt in the coping process. When aggression, neglect, or abuse become part of the family's rules and norms for interacting, a hurtful family environment may develop, which can deplete important coping resources such as self-esteem at the individual level and family satisfaction at the family level (Vangelisti et al., 2007), adding stress to an already distressed family system.

Because children learn coping and communication strategies from their parents, a hurtful family environment may also teach children that behaviors such as withdrawal and aggression are permissible coping responses to stress (Socha & Yingling, 2010). As the family heads into crisis, this vicious cycle is likely to continue until outside help is sought (Boss, 2002).

In the case of adaptation or bonadaptation, when family functioning is at a similar or better level than it was before the stressor event happened, improved family communication can be a long-term outcome of the coping process. Given that family communication is an often-cited component of family resilience, it makes sense that families notice that their interactions have improved as a result of growing from a stressful experience. According to Patterson (1988), bonadaptation is characterized, in part, by the maintenance of a family unit that can still communicate effectively to accomplish its tasks and remain committed to one another. For instance, Afifi and Keith (2004) suggest that family communication factors such as degree of interparental conflict and amount/quality of contact with the noncustodial parent can lead to either adaptive or maladaptive responses to the loss of an intact family: children do best in families where both parents spend quality time with the children and refrain from hostile conflict with each other. Indeed, positive co-parental communication and continued contact in the form of everyday talk and attendance at activities between a child and the noncustodial parent help the various family relationships remain strong or even grow in this new family form.

Summary

In this chapter, you read about the various roles of communication in the coping process. You were introduced to a communication-based model that specifies how communication serves as a source or symptom of stress, a way for families to make sense of stressful situations, an important coping resource, a means to cope with stress, and an indication of family functioning throughout the coping process. The model also helped to organize communication scholarship that falls within the various parts of the model. Whereas some areas have enjoyed a wealth of communication research with room to explore (stressor, strategy, and resource), other areas are ripe for further research to examine the connections proposed in the chapter (symptom, meaning-making, outcome). Within this discussion, you read about a theoretically driven typology that classifies various coping strategies according to their form (behavioral and cognitive approach strategies vs avoidance strategies), function (problem-focused, emotion-focused, meaning-focused, relationship-focused, and maintenance-focused coping), and level (individual, social, and communal). Although examples of communicative coping can be found throughout the matrix, it plays a central role when families use communal and social methods of coping and attempt to regulate and maintain relationships in times of stress. This chapter sets the stage for the remaining three chapters, where you will read about specific stressors families may face in two unpredictable stressors (military family separation during a wartime deployment and catastrophic illness in the form of maternal breast cancer) and one developmental stressor (transition to parenthood).

Part II

———

Family Stress and Coping in Context

In Part II, you will get the opportunity to examine communication, stress, and coping in three specific situations: geographic separation from family members (Chapter 5), catastrophic illness (Chapter 6), and the transition to parenthood (Chapter 7). These three chapters are organized in a similar way. First, you will read research that documents the stressors families face in a particular situation, as well as the individual, social, and communal coping strategies they use to contend with stress. Within this research, it is possible to identify communication practices, family characteristics, environmental and social conditions, coping resources, and coping strategies that differentiate resilient families from those that have a more difficult time adapting and adjusting to these stressful situations. Then, you will read a case study of a fictional family that has "experienced" the stressor. Although these cases are fictional, they are based on stories and narratives from existing research, my own personal and professional experiences, and stories that friends, family, and colleagues have shared with me. Each chapter concludes with a summary, sample analysis, and series of questions to help you apply the research you read in Chapters 1 through 4 to analyze the stress and coping processes of each family.

5

Stress and Coping during a Wartime Deployment

It was about the 3-week mark when little Annie, who was 3 at the time, very resolutely got dressed one morning, and it was about 20 to 30 minutes before we were supposed to be leaving the house for school and everything. She was looking for her shoes, then she was by the front door, and I said, "Baby, what are you doing?" and she's like "I'm getting ready," and I said, "That's terrific, but we're not, we're not ready to leave yet." She goes, "Oh no, I'm getting ready and I'm going to go find the blue bus." I said, "Oh babe, what are you going to do when you find the blue bus?" And she said, "I'm getting on it, and I'm going to go get papa."

I think once we were able to deal with time in terms of months, like I've made it a month, then you start going into the two-month mark. I noticed that with other spouses too, you always knew a newbee when they were talking about days, "Oh my husband has been gone for 17 days," and you just thought, oh they're still in the bad place. Then if somebody was to talk in weeks, you know in terms of weeks, oh he's been gone for four weeks, five weeks, you knew they were reaching a better level. But when somebody was finally talking in terms of months, oh they've been gone X amount months, like usually at that two-month mark, [that's] when we were just getting our pace and our pattern.

You'd see a friend of yours in black, and you're like, did I not get the notice on the funeral, you know what I mean? I'm being very callous, but I remember having a couple of conversations, seeing moms and I'm like "Oh is there a funeral today that I didn't get the notice about?" Sometimes the answer was "yes" and sometimes was "no." And then having to make decisions, do I attend the funeral of someone I don't know? That was a constant reminder, that there was obviously somebody's very real life challenges and tragedies going on all the time. It was never going away. It was a scab that was constantly being picked. –

Carol, mother of 5.

Separation from loved ones is a fact of life for many families. Although geographic separation can be a "normal" part of the family lifecycle, particularly when a child goes away to college, it can also result from unpredictable and stressful situations, such as a wartime military deployment, job loss, or incarceration (Stafford, 2005). A number of relational and family scholars study physical separation in close relationships, focusing on such situations as long-distance dating relationships (e.g., Maguire, 2007; Sahlstein, 2006), commuter marriages (e.g., Bergen et al., 2007), and nonresidential parenting (e.g., Bailey, 2003; Braithwaite & Baxter, 2006).

Similarly, a long tradition of research has focused on stress in military families. Indeed, much of the work on family resilience began with investigations of how families cope with wartime deployment (Hill, 1949; McCubbin & Patterson, 1983), one of the biggest stressors a military family can face (Wiens & Boss, 2006). Wartime deployment not only requires the service members to be separated from their families, often for a year or more; it also increases the deployed service member's risk of physical or emotional injury, capture and imprisonment, or even death (Knox & Price, 1999) – a circumstance that takes its toll on marriages and families (Wiens & Boss, 2006). Even after reunion, military families may continue to struggle as service members contend with their time at war, particularly if they experience post-traumatic stress disorder (Ray & Vanstone, 2009).

This is the first of three chapters in which you will read about stress and coping in specific contexts. In this chapter, you will read about stress and coping in military families separated during wartime. Although some scholars have studied military service members (e.g., Adler, Huffman, Castro, & Bliese, 2005), this chapter focuses on military spouses and families left behind during the deployment, because that is where the bulk of the family stress and coping research resides. The case study in this chapter is based on interviews my research partner, Erin Sahlstein, and I conducted with women whose husbands deployed to Iraq or Afghanistan between 2003 and 2005. The quotes at the start of the chapter were from one of the participants, "Carol," who experienced a number of stressors as a result of her husband's deployment, and developed a number of coping strategies to help her deal with the situation.

The Military Context

In order to understand what military families must contend with during a wartime deployment, it is important to start by examining the broader cultural context in which the family is situated – the military culture. For the purposes of this chapter, *culture* refers to "a socially constructed and historically transmitted pattern of symbols, meanings, premises, and rules" (Philipsen, 1992, p. 7). The US military fulfills many of the definitional aspects of culture: It is "learned (via socialization training such as boot camp), broadly shared by its members (e.g., saluting fellow members), and symbolic in nature (e.g., rank insignia and language jargon make sense only within a military context)" (Dunivin, 1994, p. 533). Lt Colonel Karen Dunivin, a military sociologist who was in the US Air Force, describes the traditional US military culture as "combat, warrior-masculine," and characterizes it as having a conservative, moralistic ideology that promotes exclusionary laws (the recently repealed ban on openly gay Americans serving in the US military, the somewhat limited role for women) and homogeneity among its membership. Although the US military shows signs of becoming more egalitarian and open to multiple perspectives, Dunivin (1994) states that the "military still views itself as *the* primary instrument of national power whose combat missions, performed by masculine warriors, characterizes its very existence and meaning" (p. 537).

According to James Burke (as cited in Snider, 1999), the

central elements of the military culture derive from "an attempt to deal with (and, if possible to overcome) the uncertainty of war, to impose some pattern on war, to control war's outcome, and to invest war with meaning and significance" (p. 15). Using Hofstede's (2001) dimensions of cultural differences among countries, Soeters and colleagues (Soeters, Poponote, & Page, 2006) described several cultural differences between the military and civilian organizations that help to characterize these central elements of the military culture:

> In the military, hierarchies and power distances are known to be more elaborate and fundamental to the structure of the organization than they are in the business sector. In the military, collectivism (i.e., group orientation, interdependency, and cohesion) is clearly a more important concept than it is among average civilian organizations. In the military, finally, earning high salaries and striving for individual merit is not valued as much as in business corporations.
>
> (p. 16)

Given the importance of indoctrinating new military service members to these ideals, it is no surprise that the ideals of collectivism, authority, and control influence military families as well. Indeed, Knox and Price (1999) described how the military culture affects family life, particularly for career military families:

> [T]he culture profoundly affects – in many ways restricts – the activities and behaviors of spouses and children who are expected to be as committed to the military lifestyle and mission as the military member. Family member dedication is expected of a career military family. Active spousal and family member involvement in the culture is interpreted as a sign of commitment and adaption to military life. The cultural imperative imposed upon every military member, active or reserve, is contact preparedness to do his or her job . . . The mission imperative demands that the family members go along with the requirements placed upon themselves when the military member is absent while carrying out his or her duty. Normal lifecycle family demands may go unattended by the military member and be attended solely by the family.
>
> (p. 129)

Situated in this somewhat cloistered existence, military families experience many stressors unique to military family life, including frequent separations and reunions, regimentation and conformity to military life, separation from the nonmilitary community, frequent relocation (for active-duty families), and a structured and hierarchically organized social system (Norwood, Fullerton, & Hagen, 1996). Because they do not live within the military culture full-time, reservists and their families are somewhat protected from the effect of military life on the family, although their isolation from military communities produces additional stressors, such as unfamiliarity with accessing military benefits and being "left out of" military social support networks (Faber, Willerton, Clymer, MacDermid, & Weiss, 2008). The added stress of a wartime deployment, which includes danger, uncertainty, and prolonged separation, can push active-duty and reserve families over the edge, leaving members at risk of negative mental, emotional, or even physical health consequences (Flake, Davis, Johnson, & Middleton, 2009; Wright, Burrell, Schroeder, & Thomas, 2006)

The Family and Wartime Deployment

According to Wiens and Boss (2006), military deployments are "defining experiences for military service members and their families. They are one of the most widely documented stressors for military families" (p. 13). Indeed, research has revealed a number of negative mental, emotional, and physical effects that deployment of a loved one to a combat zone has on military families, such as the loss of companionship and parental support, increased risk of divorce, increased spousal and child maltreatment, and higher incidences of depression and anxiety among family members (Flake et al., 2009; Karney & Crown, 2007; McFarlane, 2009; Palmer, 2008; Wiens & Boss, 2006). Risk factors include lack of unit affiliation (which may be common for reserve or National Guard families), newness to the military system, inexperience with wartime deployment, and the presence of additional stressors, challenges, or traumas (Wiens & Boss, 2006). At the same time, successful adaptation to the deployment can benefit military families by increasing their resilience (Wiens & Boss, 2006), depending on the stressors the family faces, the coping resources available to them, and the coping strategies they use. Individual family members such as the non-deployed spouse also report benefits of a deployment, including an increased sense of independence and not taking the marriage for granted (Maguire & Sahlstein, 2011). Indeed, some research suggests that military marriages can actually improve as a result of a deployment (Drummet, Coleman, & Cable, 2003). Despite these benefits, deployment is still a time period full of uncertainty and stress for military families.

Stressors

Military families face stress from a number of different sources during a wartime deployment. Whereas some are unrelated to (but are exacerbated by) the deployment, others are directly tied to the experience. A number of stressors have already been outlined, particularly those associated with military life. In addition, military families still experience both the predictable (such as the birth of a child) and the unpredictable (such as an automobile accident) stressors that emerge over the course of a family's lifecycle. When stressors such as these start to "pile up" or happen simultaneously, military families are at additional risk of distress (Weins & Boss, 2006). In the case of a wartime deployment, where military families experience different stressors depending on the phase of a deployment (Maguire & Sahlstein, 2011), it is important to discuss stressors according to the three phases of the deployment cycle: pre-deployment, deployment, and reunion.

Pre-Deployment

The pre-deployment phase starts when the family is notified of the impending deployment and ends when the service member leaves the family for the actual mission. Military families may respond with a marked level of tension, protest, or even anger in the first couple of weeks after notification, particularly if they are given insufficient time (a month or less) to adjust to the service member's impending departure (Moelker & van der Kloet, 2006). Wiens and Boss (2006) characterize this stage as a time when service members are physically present but psychologically absent, because they are busy preparing for the deployment. This can serve as a source of stress for military families, who may feel bitter that their family member is already becoming "distant" because of his or her increased workload. During the pre-deployment period families may experience increased stress from problems with social network members who fail to offer good support, and an early sense of loss as they anticipate the service member's departure (Maguire & Sahlstein, 2011). Children of parents who are about to deploy may also experience emotional withdrawal, apathy, or aggression (Flake et al., 2009). Family members often feel uncertainty surrounding deployment logistics (such as the location or length of the deployment) and how the deployment could affect marital and family relationships (Sahlstein et al., 2009). Emotionally, the period just before separation can be especially stressful, often entailing mutual withdrawal, increased fighting, and talks about the family's future (Norwood et al., 1996).

Deployment

During the separation phase, the service member is physically absent but psychologically present in the home, which leads to complicated emotional responses (Wiens & Boss, 2006). Upon separation, relational partners experience a wide range of emotions, such as anger, loss, loneliness, and feelings of abandonment (Norwood et al., 1996). This period of emotional disorganization is relatively short-lived, lasting up to 6 weeks, but may continue if problems arise (Moelker & van der Kloet, 2006). The intensity of these emotions also varies with the length of separation and level of uncertainty surrounding the separation. As time goes on, these negative emotions can give way to positive emotions, such as hope, confidence, and calmness (Rotter & Boveja, 1999), as the family "gets used" to the new situation. Indeed, families often report feeling a sense of relief when the deployment has begun as they begin the adjustment process (Maguire & Sahlstein, 2011). Then again, many children act out during the deployment and display minor to serious behavioral problems, such as anxiety or aggression – although they, too, enter their own readjustment phase, when such problems may diminish (Flake et al., 2009). As the time for reunion approaches, the couple begins to anticipate being together again. This time is characterized by feelings of excitement about the reunion as well as worry about being together again (Norwood et al., 1996).

During separation, the family faces a number of stressors: psychological (periodic worry, sadness, loneliness during a dangerous deployment), logistical (finding out how to communicate with the deployed service member, taking care of household needs and children, renegotiating boundaries and family roles), social (unhelpful support from network members, media reports of negative events where the deployed member is stationed), relational (role struggles), and economic (rearranging employment) (Drummet et al., 2003; Maguire & Sahlstein, 2011; Sahlstein et al., 2009; Wadsworth, 2010). Ironically, military families report stress during service members' return to their families during their two-week rest and recuperation breaks as well, often as a result of unfulfilled expectations: for example, the family makes plans for the break, but all the service member wants to do is sleep (Maguire & Sahlstein, 2011). In regard to the wars in Iraq and Afghanistan, a survey of military families conducted for the National Military Family Association (NMFA) (2005) revealed a number of other sources of stress including long separations (over a year), a greater frequency of deployments, and an increased OPTEMPO (the pace of preparing for a military operation) for service members. Service members and their spouses also report stress over whether their partners will remain faithful during the separation (Maguire & Sahlstein, 2011; McNulty, 2005).

Reunion

When the deployment is over and the service member returns, family members experience a sense of euphoria as they talk to one another and reestablish intimacy. After this honeymoon is over, however, the family begins the process of renegotiating the relationship and redefining roles (Norwood et al., 1996). This period can be one of the most stressful times for military families, even more so than the separation, because they must figure out how to renegotiate relational roles, together time, and tasks (Flake et al., 2009). During the reunion phase, service members are physically "back home" but may remain psychologically distant from their spouses and/or children as they cope with their own wartime experiences (Wiens & Boss, 2006). This contradiction is evident as military families struggle with decisions regarding what to disclose about the deployment and what to conceal (Sahlstein et al., 2009). Eventually, the family regains a "new" sense of normalcy as it becomes reintegrated after separation (Moelker & van der Kloet, 2006). Commonly cited reunion stressors include role and boundary strain, giving up independence and relinquishing tasks to the returning family member, withdrawal from social support networks, children's rejection of the returning parent, and changes in the physical and/or mental condition of the returning service member, including post-traumatic stress disorder (Drummet et al., 2003; Maguire & Sahlstein, 2011; Wadsworth, 2010).

Resources

Successful adaptation to a wartime deployment depends on resources such as flexible gender roles, active coping strategies, a sense of togetherness and family coherence, and shared family values (McCubbin & Patterson, 1983; Wiens & Boss, 2006). Family communication is another important resource, because it allows military families to express their emotions and solve problems, and it helps them keep track of one another's daily experiences during separation and adapt to living together after the separation is over (Hill, 1949; Norwood et al., 1996; Yerkes

& Holloway, 1996). One of the most important resources at a family's disposal during a wartime deployment is social support (McCubbin & Patterson, 1983; Wiens & Boss, 2006). According to Drummet et al. (2003), "Military families need social support to cope with separation stressors," particularly from friends, extended family, work colleagues, church members, and support groups (p. 282). The military subculture has a rich tradition of strong interpersonal relationships among spouses and active duty military families supporting one another during deployments, likely owing to its collectivistic orientation (McCubbin, 1979; Montalvo, 1976).

Whereas many of the families form bonds on their own, other families find value in the family support programs that the military offers. For instance, the Army has family readiness groups (FRGs), command-sponsored organizations that "act as an extension of the unit in providing official, accurate command information, provide mutual support between the command and the FRG membership, advocate more efficient use of community resources, [and] help families solve problems at the lowest level" (US Army FRG Leader's Handbook, 2010, p. 11). FRG leaders, who are often officers' spouses, are expected to perform duties ranging from identifying problems within families that might negatively affect soldiers' ability to fulfill their missions to providing support during family crises (such as financial problems or the death of a soldier). Whereas some research shows that family readiness for a deployment resulting from FRG activities relates to improved family well-being and soldier productivity (NMFA, 2004; Orthner & Rose, 2003), other research shows that FRGs can promote stress among members (Di Nola, 2008). In a study of Army wives' perceptions of FRGs, Sahlstein and Maguire (2011) found that the rank of the husband (officer vs enlisted) divided the FRG, leading some members to feel committed to the group whereas others felt alienated from the group or felt that the support was not adequate. Their study also showed that FRGs are stressful for leaders when they are left without the support they need to run the group, thereby sapping their time and energy and depleting them of their own resources for coping effectively with the deployment.

Coping Strategies and Outcomes

Military families adapt successfully to stress by developing a range of coping behaviors, from maintaining family stability and individual anxiety, to getting support from family, friends, and the community (McCubbin, 1979). Many descriptive, analytical, and prescriptive articles discuss how military families can and should cope with wartime deployment at the individual, social, and communal levels. Most of the studies have focused on the coping strategies of military spouses, often the wives; few, if any, focus on the coping strategies that children employ. A sample of these strategies is offered in Table 5.1, using the matrix presented in Chapter 4. The only strategy that was not clearly identified in the literature was a communal-level, meaning-focused cognition, likely because there is limited military family research on meaning-focused coping (Dimiceli et al., 2010).

Research consistently points to several key coping strategies most closely associated with family resilience or successful adaptation to deployment. Boss (2002) highlights two coping strategies as important factors in family resilience during wartime deployment: establishing independence and self-sufficiency by the remaining parent, and maintaining family integrity (p. 80). Patterson and McCubbin (1984) studied the specific coping responses of distressed and non-distressed Navy couples separated during an eight-month deployment, using the Coping with Separation Inventory (McCubbin, Boss, Wilson, & Lester, 1980). Results indicated that the wives in non-distressed couples used the strategies of believing in the lifestyle and optimism (perceiving the benefits of the spouse's profession and having faith in God and the future) and developing self-reliance and self-esteem more than distressed couples. In addition, the non-distressed wives used a wider variety of coping strategies than the distressed couples. Furthermore, research suggests that problem-focused coping efforts are associated with increased well-being, whereas emotion-focused efforts are often associated with a decrease in well-being (Dimiceli et al., 2010). Communication with the deployed service member has been cited as an important coping strategy as well

Table 5.1. A Sample of Coping Strategies Used as Families Face a Wartime Deployment.

		Problem-Focused	Emotion-Focused	Meaning-Focused	Relationship-Focused	Maintenance-Focused
Behavior	*Individual*	Solve own problems[1]	Cry[2]	Keep a journal[3]	Do partner's chores[5]	Send care packages[3]
	Social	Learn about deployment from FRG[2]	Talk to other military spouses[2]	Ask others for their opinion[7]	Help service member prepare for the deployment[2]	Spend time as a family with others in social network[3]
	Communal	Co-create a financial plan[7]	Share feelings with each other[2]	Discuss benefits of the deployment[6]	Discuss how to best communicate while apart[8]	Spend quality family time together[2]
Cognition	*Individual*	Break down a problem into pieces[6]	Think about deployment in a positive light[1]	Believe in military lifestyle[5]	Consider partner's needs[2]	Wear a symbol of the relationship (e.g., a ring)[3]
	Social	Seek advice[3]	Compare self to others in past wars[3]	Pray[3]	Organize family life[2]	Talk about the deployed family member to others[3]
	Communal	Create a new outlook on problems[1]	Talk about when the deployment is over[3]		Negotiate family roles and rules[2]	Keep the memory of a captured service member alive[4]

Avoidance					
Individual	Take classes[7]	Seek an escape via distractions[2]	Pretend it will not happen[1]	Avoid conflict[2]	Establish autonomy from partner[4]
Social	Focus attention on other families[2]	Refrain from watching the news[2]	Blame the military[6]	Withhold information to protect deployed member[2]	Develop friendships outside the family[3]
Communal	Stay away from military environment[7]	Talk about anything but the deployment[2]	Deny the possibility of death/injury[1]	Create psychological distance between each other[2]	Isolate family time from outsiders [2]

Source: 1 = Dimiceli et al., 2010; 2 = Maguire & Sahlstein, 2011; 3 = Merolla, 2010; 4 = Boss (2002); 5 = McCubbin et al., 1980; 6 = Hobfoll et al. 1991; 7 = McCubbin, Dahl, & Hunter, 1976; 8 = Drummet et al., 2003.

because it serves to maintain family integrity and helps service members and their families adjust to separation and reunion (Hill, 1949; Drummet et al., 2003; Wiens & Boss, 2006). Finally, Orthner and Rose (2003) found that families with high separation adjustment reported comfort in dealing with Army agencies. They also spent quality time together, did volunteer work, and received support from friends, neighbors, and relatives.

Case Study

As is evident in the first part of this chapter, military deployment takes a heavy toll on military families and the members who serve. With adequate resources and a flexible, extensive coping reper-toire, military families can emerge from a deployment not merely intact, but stronger and more resilient than before. Although reading the research gives you some appreciation for what these families experience, one of the best ways to learn about family stress and coping during wartime deployment (or any stressful situation) is to read case studies: first-hand accounts of families who have actually lived through a deployment. Like any story, a case presents a conflict, typically the tension between alternative courses of action that bring different viewpoints, interests, and values into contention and that must be resolved by a decision (Braithwaite & Wood, 2000). In this chapter, you as the reader have the opportunity to analyze this tension and assess how well the family coped with wartime deployment. I also offer an inter-pretation of the case at the end of the chapter to help guide you in the process.

Although military spouses have written a number of books giving witness to their experiences – books such as *365 Deployment Days: A Wife's Survival Story* by Sara Dawalt (2007), *Life After Deployment: Military Families Share Reunion Stories and Advice* by Karen Pavlicin (2007), and *While They're at War* by Kristin Henderson (2006) – the case study in this chapter comes from my own research on stress and coping during a long-term wartime deployment. My research partner and I interviewed 50 women whose husbands had deployed to either Iraq or Afghanistan

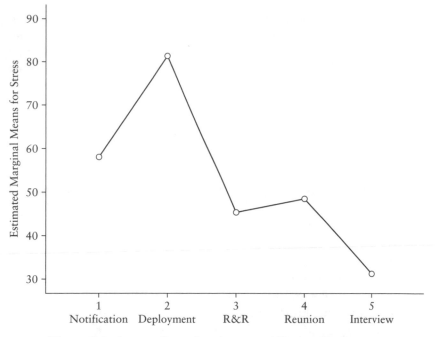

Figure 5.1: Average Stress Level across a Wartime Deployment

between 2003 and 2005. The average participant was 32 years old, had been married for seven years, and had two children. We asked the participants to recall the period of time starting at notification of their most recent deployment and ending with the time of the interview, and to report the significant events, or turning points, during that time frame. During each deployment phase, participants reported the sources of stress they experienced, their communication patterns with their husbands (how often they talked, what modes of communication they used), and how they coped with their stress.

We also asked them to chart their personal stress level at each turning point, ranging from 0% to 100%. The graph in Figure 5.1 represents the average stress levels for the participants at five points in time: notification, deployment, rest and recuperation (R&R) visit, reunion, and the time of the interview. As you can see, stress was at a fairly high level during pre-deployment, peaked during the deployment, and then decreased until the reunion, where we see a small increase in stress once more until it bottomed out at the time of the interview. The case you are about to read mirrors this graph as it is a compilation of the stories our participants told us during the interviews. Although the case itself is fictional, many of the specific stressors and coping methods you will read about are true and often in the women's own words.

Case Overview

Rashelle and Peter Sherman, both 32, have been married for twelve years and have two children: Marcus, 8, and Malea, 6. Rashelle works at a local advertising agency, and Peter is an engineer who serves in the Army reserves. They have a tight-knit family that values open and honest communication, often having "family meetings" to discuss issues that affect the family. A common topic of discussion during family meetings is what Rashelle and the kids should do when Peter fulfills his reserve duty one weekend a month and two weeks out of the year. During the weekend absences, Rashelle and the kids do their own "training" program through outings to the zoo, the local nature reserve, or the amusement park in a nearby town. During the longer absences, they travel out of town to visit family. When Peter's unit was deployed to Afghanistan for one year, however, the family began to fall apart as Rashelle struggled to be a "single" parent balancing career, motherhood, and her own fears for her husband.

Pre-deployment. Rashelle stepped back to admire the work she had done in her daughter's room. She wanted Malea to have a special place to go during the upcoming winter months, and thought the garden theme gave her the perfect escape. She heard Peter come into the room and sit calmly on the floor. As she turned back to put some additional touches on the mural she had painted, she said, "I love this new room, but I think we need to buy a new bed to go with the room's theme. I know that will be expensive, but I think it will be worth it, don't you?" When she didn't hear a response, she turned and saw that look on Peter's face that always caused her to panic.

"I'm going to Afghanistan," Peter said.

"Are you serious???" replied Rashelle, as she dropped the paintbrush and walked up to Peter. "When do you leave?"

Peter answered, "It looks like my unit will be officially activated next week. When that happens, I have to leave for six weeks of training at Fort Bragg in North Carolina. I'll come back for a couple of weeks, then we are supposed to leave December 1st."

Rashelle didn't know quite what to do, say, or think. She had known it was a possibility, but in the back of her mind, she just didn't think they would have to go through a deployment now that things were beginning to look up in Afghanistan. As she began thinking about all the things they would need to do to get ready, her eyes landed on a picture of her, Peter, and the kids at Disneyland. It was such a happy time, and it was clear how much the kids adored their dad. How were they going to tell the children? "We should wait to tell the kids," she decided. "I'd hate to get them all upset only to find you aren't going anywhere. You know the Army – one thing we can count on is that they will change their minds."

"I was thinking the same thing," said Peter. At that moment, instead of running into Peter's arms, she turned back around, picked up the brush, and resumed painting the mural. Peter sat a few more minutes, then got up and left the room.

A few days later, when Rashelle went to pick up the kids, she had a hard time keeping her cool. They were hanging out with their friends, even when they saw the car approaching. "Marcus, Malea, get in the car NOW! I don't want to wait here all day while you yack with your friends." At this, the kids sighed, waved goodbye to their buddies, and got into the car.

When they got home, the kids went to find their dad, knowing he was usually home early that day so he could play Wii with them. They found him in the TV room, with a new game already cued up. "Awesome! You got us Total Chaos IV! I thought we couldn't get it!" exclaimed Marcus.

"Well, I decided, 'why not?' and got it anyway. Y'all ready to get annihilated?" The kids ran to their dad, with Malea taking one control and Marcus the other so the battle could begin.

As Rashelle stood in the doorway watching her husband and children play together, she could see in a flash all the moments that her husband would miss. Some parents don't want to spend time with their kids, but Peter loved spending time with them, loved playing with them. He probably wouldn't be here for Marcus's birthday because of training, and would likely miss Malea's school science fair competition. Then there was Christmas. At that point, she started crying and quickly left the room, but not before Malea saw her leave.

Malea followed her mom to the kitchen and asked, "What's wrong, Mommy? Are you and dad getting a divorce? I heard you fighting last night."

It was then that Rashelle realized she and Peter would need to talk with the kids. She could no longer deny the reality of what was about to happen. "No, honey," she said. "I'll . . . we'll be alright."

After dinner, when the family usually spent time together doing dishes and cleaning up, Rashelle and Peter called a family meeting to tell the kids about the deployment.

"Are you going to die, Daddy?" asked Malea, her eyes welling up with tears.

"I'm going to do my best not to, Peanut," he replied, giving her a reassuring hug.

"But you're gonna miss my birthday!" moaned Marcus as he grabbed one of his toy soldiers and started fiddling with it. "You promised you'd teach me how to ride my bike!"

"I can do that, honey," said Rashelle, trying her best to look calm and confident.

"That's not your job, that's Daddy's job!" Marcus yelled as he stormed out of the room, quickly followed by Malea, who ran to her bedroom and slammed the door. Peter and Rashelle looked at each other, sighed, and went to their room as well. They spent the next several hours hugging each other, talking about their fears, making plans for the deployment, and saying all the things they should have been saying the day he found out.

The day of departure. When Peter first told Rashelle about the deployment, it sounded like things would be happening pretty fast, but when Peter got back from training, the Army kept changing his deployment date. First it was December 1st, then the 15th, and finally January 5th . . . or so they thought. Although it was good that they got to spend the holidays together, there was a damper on the celebration with the deployment looming over their heads, and the waiting and changing dates were driving Rashelle crazy. The last straw came when on the morning of the 5th: as Rashelle and the kids were helping to put Peter's things in the car, a call came in from Peter's sergeant, stating that once again there was a delay, and that they would be leaving two days later. Before, when the dates changed, they would celebrate with a family dinner at a nice restaurant. Now, Rashelle wanted off the roller coaster; even the kids were done. Peter tried to cheer everyone up, and suggested that they go out to eat that night, but Rashelle lost her appetite and said he could go with just the kids. The kids even said no, that they would rather eat at home and go to bed early. Peter was hurt, but understood that his family was tired of all the changes.

When the time finally came, Peter and Rashelle decided that the kids should go to school, even though their dad was deploying, just to maintain a sense of normalcy. Before he walked out the door, Peter gave a hug and a kiss to the kids, just as he always did before going to work, and got into the car with Rashelle to go to the airport. After many hugs and tears, Peter finally entered the terminal, leaving Rashelle on the curb. When she got in the car, instead of breaking down into tears, she just started laughing. She laughed and laughed, feeling this bizarre sense of happiness and relief. She had dreaded this moment for so long, and now that it had finally happened, she felt this huge weight had been lifted from her. She could now look forward to getting on with her new life as a single mom, hoping the months would fly.

Deployment. The first few weeks after the deployment were rough. Rashelle is normally an organized person, and has no problem taking care of the kids and doing her job. She hadn't realized how much Peter had done around the house until he was gone. Now, Rashelle was lucky to get the kids out the door in time to make the bus. She also had difficulty getting off work early enough so she could be at home with the kids on Fridays as Peter had done. She wished she had someone else around to help her out, and was missing her mom and dad, who lived 300 miles away.

When they first found out about the deployment, Rashelle called her parents in hopes that they would be able to come out and visit in the early weeks of the deployment. Unfortunately, her father fell while working on the house and hurt his back, delaying their visit. Rashelle's sister, who lived 30 miles away, was supposed to take a week off work to help, but she had to cancel because her 7-year-old son, Tommy, got the flu. Rashelle knew it wasn't anyone's fault, but she still felt frustrated that her family couldn't help. Rashelle's only salvation was her team at work. They were not only her colleagues but her friends as well. Even though none of them had ever experienced a deployment, they supported her – letting her vent and picking up the slack when she needed to leave early or come in late. Her boss was wonderful, too, and was willing to work with her and her schedule as long as the team accomplished their goals. After about two months, Rashelle finally worked out a system that seemed to appease everyone.

In all her efforts to balance work and household responsibilities, Rashelle didn't pay much attention to the kids. They were usually quite self-sufficient, doing their homework without being told, cleaning their room, and helping around the house. They were both "A" students and enjoyed school. While Malea continued getting good grades, Marcus's grades started slipping, to the point where he might need to take summer school. Rashelle tried to talk to Marcus, but he would only say, "I'll try, Mom," and fiddle with the toy soldier.

It all came to a head one day when Rashelle got a call at work from the school. "Mrs Sherman? This is Ms Peterson from the Wayne School. We just wanted to check and see if Marcus was OK, because he didn't show up for school today."

"Excuse me," said Rashelle, "but I saw him get on the bus this morning. There must be some kind of mistake."

"There's no mistake. His teacher, Mr Smith, said he didn't come to class this morning."

Rashelle hung up the phone, told her boss what had happened, and without thinking, sent an email to Peter telling him what was going on. It said, "Hi. Marcus didn't show up for school today. I'm going to look for him. Will keep you posted."

She was frantic. Where could he be? She called all of his friends' parents, but none of them knew where he was. She went to the house, the park, the theater, but there was no sign of him. She finally called the police to report that her son was missing. A car came out to the house, and two police officers took her statement. They also asked for a recent picture of Marcus, as well as a sample of his hair.

"Why do you want that?" she asked.

"We need it in case we need to make an identification," said the officer.

At that point, Rashelle completely broke down. It wasn't enough to have to worry about her husband all the time. Now, her son was missing. She didn't think she could face this situation by herself, so she called her parents and asked them to come down to help in the search. They said they would be there in a few hours. Rashelle was about to call her FRG leader to find out how to bring Peter home in case there was trouble when her cell phone rang. It was her sister.

"Hi Shelle. Missing someone?"

Rashelle paused, then said, "Is Marcus with you?"

"Yes, he is. Don't worry, he's fine. He must have caught the city bus to our house from the school. I'm glad he remembered where we keep the spare key. You can imagine my surprise when I saw his smiling face when Tommy and I got home."

Awash with relief, Rashelle thanked her sister, asked her to call their parents so they wouldn't have to make the drive, arranged for a sitter for Malea, and drove to get Marcus.

When she finally got to bed that night, she was exhausted. Her talk with Marcus didn't go as well as she had hoped. She was so angry about what he did that she didn't stop to ask him why he went to his aunt's house. She just yelled at him, grounded him for two weeks, and sent him to his room. She was just about to fall asleep when the phone rang.

"Hello?" she said, feeling that fear when the phone rings late at night.

"It's me. I just finished talking to my commanding officer, and he said I can come home since it is so close to R&R. We'll find him, I promise," said Peter in a rush.

"Oh, crap!" said Rashelle. "I totally forgot to send you another email. Marcus went to Rebecca's house. He's fine."

Relieved but frustrated, Peter said he was glad he was safe, but wished she would have let him know sooner, because he had been in a panic all day.

Rashelle felt guilty, but angry too. "What was I supposed to do? Wait until he came up dead to let you know?"

At that point, Peter said, "I have to go. We'll talk about this when I come home," and hung up the phone.

Rashelle was glad he would be home for R&R, but was also worried, because the call didn't bode well for their visit. Instead of sleeping, she spent the rest of the night cleaning up the house as she usually did when she couldn't sleep.

R&R: A glimpse of the future? The time had finally come for Peter's two-week R&R. Marcus's "trip" to his aunt's house was a distant memory as Rashelle and the kids cleaned the house, mowed the lawn, and prepared the surprise party for Peter. Rashelle invited all their friends and family to welcome him home and help him decompress from six months in Afghanistan. She had also made other plans for the family. The kids were off school for the summer, so there was plenty of time for some good, quality family time. But despite all her planning, reality got in the way.

First, Peter's plane was 6 hours late getting in, making the surprise party a wash. Next, instead of wanting to go out and do things with the family, all Peter wanted to do was sleep. Even when he finally did leave the house, he wasn't much fun, and the kids were disappointed that their playmate was so withdrawn. He wasn't even interested in the little black nighty Rashelle had bought. Rashelle thought to herself, "Oh no, there's something wrong with us. We should be happy, but we're not. What if he's found someone in Afghanistan? After all, there are a lot of female soldiers now . . ." She quickly dismissed the thought, however, because she didn't think he would really cheat on her.

Then, there was Monopoly night.

The night before Peter was to return to Afghanistan, Rashelle's parents, sister, nephew, and the rest of the family went out to dinner, then came back to the house to visit. Finally, the kids went to bed about 11:00, and the relatives left. Instead of going to bed, Peter and Rashelle decided to play a game of Monopoly to soak up as much time together as they could. But instead of having fun, they ended up fighting. Their communication hadn't been very good during R&R, and it all seemed to come to a head during the game. Finally, at 2:30 in the morning, Peter said, "Rashelle, I'm done. Enough with this arguing! I'm gonna leave in like five hours and I need to rest. I can't do this anymore." As he walked out of the room, Rashelle started crying and curled up on the couch in the family room.

Two hours later, Rashelle decided she needed to make things right. She crawled into their bed and said, "I'm so sorry. I love you so much. I don't want you to leave."

Peter pulled her to him and said, "I don't want to leave either. I can't go back there." They spent the next two hours pouring out their feelings of fear and frustration to the point that they were finally able to sleep for an hour before they had to go to the airport. After Rashelle dropped Peter off and said her goodbyes, she got into the car, and instead of laughter, tears came pouring down her face. She was glad they had made things right before he left; nevertheless, she had a bad feeling that when they were finally together again after the deployment, problems would continue. She also vowed never to play Monopoly again.

Case Analysis

The Shermans experienced many of the stressors identified in the military family research, some of which involved communication and/or relational issues. For example, Rashelle felt frustrated when her family members were unable to help during the first few weeks of the deployment. Even though she appraised the situation as out of her family's control, she also saw their absence as a threat to her own "coping plan," leaving her with depleted coping resources and thus more vulnerable to stress. She also felt stress related to relational uncertainty, because she was unsure whether her marriage would survive the deployment, based on their negative experience with "Monopoly night" and the changes in her husband while he was at home during R&R, both of which she perceived as threats to their relationship. What she failed to realize, however, was that their R&R experience was not unusual, and that Peter's behavior during R&R was more indicative of his own need to cope with his wartime experiences than of problems in their relationship. Indeed, one of the most important family resources the Shermans had going into the deployment was a strong sense of cohesion between and among Rashelle, Peter, and their children. This sense of cohesion may protect the family bonds during the tumultuous deployment experience.

In regard to coping, each of the family members displayed a number of different coping responses as the situation unfolded. Rashelle's first response was denial, with the belief that the deployment might not happen after all. Peter may have also been in denial, because he agreed with Rashelle to wait to tell the children about the possible deployment until they received final word. Their choice to "protect" their children from potentially distressing news during an uncertain time seemed to conflict with the family's value of open communication. The use of denial and protective buffering may indicate a larger pattern of distancing that seemed to characterize the coping of each family member (for example, Rashelle and the kids' refusing to go out to dinner with Peter upon hearing the change in deployment date; Peter's decision to hang up the phone instead of discussing Rashelle's choices the day Marcus ran away from home). Although this pattern may seem to contradict the family cohesion that characterized life prior to the deployment, the strong connections among family members likely contributed to their choice of coping responses: the loss of such an important member of the family resulted in a need to distance themselves emotionally from one another so they could cope with their own feelings. They also may have avoided conflict so as to protect the relationship from additional harm. Twice in the case (after they told the children and fought over Monopoly), Rashelle and Peter were able to have productive, relationship-affirming conversations once they released their emotions through crying, venting, or having time to "cool off." This is a positive sign that, contrary to Rashelle's fears, they may be able to survive the deployment.

Questions for Further Analysis

1. Based on what you read, what factors (if any) are present that might put the Shermans at risk of crisis?
2. In addition to the stressors discussed in the case summary, what other stressors did the Shermans experience as a result of the deployment? How did they cope with these stressors? How effective were they in the coping process? (Think about both the short- and long-term outcomes of their coping responses.)
3. According to the model presented in Chapter 4, communication plays a number of different roles in the coping process. The case analysis pointed out how communication can be a source of stress, a resource, and a coping response in the form of distancing. What about the other two roles (communication as an outcome and communication as meaning-making)?
4. Do you think Rashelle should have told Peter about Marcus's disappearance? If so, why? If not, how could she have handled it differently?
5. Thinking ahead, what issues will the Shermans likely face when Peter comes home? What could they do during the second half of the deployment to prepare for the reunion?

6

Stress and Coping during Catastrophic Illness

October 6, 2000

. . . life is about attaching and separating, setting goals and achieving them, regrouping when things don't work out . . . probably what is hardest for you right now is the conflict that dances closest: "if I really share myself with someone, they will leave and I will feel hurt". There's the secret, though. I learned about it first 15 years ago with [my friend who died], but I can't show you how to make it yours. It takes guts and trust to allow the intimacy and know that, by allowing someone in, they *will* be with you forever. If you're lucky, they'll live with you. But even if you're not that lucky, they will have enriched you, and you, them. And they will be part of you forever. You say you already know this, from [friends that you have lost]. But trust comes hard. If I didn't believe it myself, I'd be chasing three dozen some people away rather than gathering them near.

. . . demand that I live another year! Go ahead. It sounds good enough that I'll demand it, too! You're there for ME, and for the rest of the family when they need you. You have presented papers and are becoming an authority in your field; you love your research; and you have a gang hugging you onward as you put together your dissertation, all cheering just as I am. Family support goes both ways, doesn't it. I love the glow in your eyes in the North Texas graduation picture; I know I'll see it again at UT. So, yell when you need to, call when you need to, cry when you need to . . . and ask help when you need to. I'm struggling, too, but I'm no longer afraid of the dance. We can take turns being leader, you and I. Neither of us has any idea what will happen next week, or in two months, or next year. Me? I'm dancing as fast as I can. And I think you are, too. I love you.

These are excerpts from a letter that I received a few days after my mother died of a rare form of cancer. Unbeknown to me, she had written the letter after one of our regular phone calls, five months before her death, when we talked about my worry for her and fear of starting a new relationship in a time of great chaos. During my mother's 18-month battle with cancer, I not only had to cope with the real possibility of losing my mother, but also with comprehensive exams, a dissertation, and a new-found romance. To say the least, I was stressed. I am fortunate to have such a gift from her; the letter helped me cope with one of the most difficult experiences of my life. Her views on relationships, stress, and coping as evidenced in these excerpts have also inspired my research regarding the role of communication throughout the coping process as families face adversity. Witnessing the effects of her death on my family also taught me, first-hand, what can happen when the "kinkeeper" of the family – the one who holds the family together – is stricken by a catastrophic illness.

One of the most significant sources of unpredictable stress that a family can face is when a loved one is affected by a catastrophic illness such as cancer. According to the Center for Disease Control (2007), cancer is the second leading cause of death for males and females of all ages. Although other cancers, such as lung cancer, colorectal cancer, prostate cancer, and childhood leukemia profoundly affect families, much of the research on how cancer affects families has focused on breast cancer, likely as a result of the funding opportunities available in the area as well as organizations such as the Susan Komen Breast Cancer Foundation and the grassroots activism of patients and survivors of the disease (Turner & West, 2006).

The attention breast cancer receives is well warranted. Breast cancer is the most common form of cancer among women, with 200,000 new cases diagnosed every year (American Cancer Society, 2010). Men can get breast cancer too, although the number of cases is much smaller: In 2010, the American Cancer Society predicted that nearly 2,000 men will be diagnosed with breast cancer, with almost 400 men expected to die as a result of the disease. Whereas breast cancer is a highly treatable disease if caught early, 15% of cancer-related deaths each year are because of breast cancer (The American Cancer Society). According to Fisher (2010), although the risk of getting breast cancer increases with age, women can contract the disease during any point in their adulthood. A diagnosis of breast cancer for a woman in her thirties may be particularly devastating, because younger women tend to have a more aggressive form of the disease. Furthermore, between 5% and 10% of breast cancer cases are thought to be hereditary. A woman's chance of getting breast cancer doubles if one of her first-degree relatives (a mother, sister, or daughter) has it, and triples if two of them have it (American Cancer Society, 2010). If she tests positive for the BRCA 1 or 2 gene mutation, her chances of contracting breast cancer are between 55% and 85% (Hughes et al., 2001).

Breast cancer is a "family disease" in many ways. Female family members whose loved one is coping with breast cancer cannot help but worry about their own chances of getting the disease, which may impair their ability to provide support. In addition, when someone is diagnosed with the disease, his or her partner and children are deeply affected by the illness. The book *Cancer in two voices* by Sandra Butler and Barbara Rosenblum (1996), for instance, chronicles how the death of a life partner profoundly affects the surviving partner and her ability to grieve. Spouses often take on new role responsibilities, such as caring for the children, completing household chores, and providing physical care and emotional support (Hilton et al., 2000). Young children are affected, too, experiencing feelings of sadness, confusion, and anger. Adolescents are at particular risk, because they are old enough to understand what is happening, yet feel pulled between the need to help their family and the desire to become independent adults (Davey et al., 2005).

Instead of focusing on rare cancers like my mother's cancer or more deadly forms of the disease such as lung cancer, this chapter focuses on breast cancer, given the extensive research it has received. Because the research on stress and coping in the context of breast cancer is extensive, a complete review of the literature is beyond the scope of this chapter. At the same time, a number of stressors, coping resources, and strategies have been repeatedly identified across multiple studies in this context; these will be the focus of the next section of this chapter. After reading the literature, you will then read a case study of a family dealing with breast cancer, based in part on stories publicly available on the website *BreastCancerStories.org*. Although my mother had a different form of cancer, I also weave in some of my own family's experiences with cancer, allowing me to offer a first-hand account of the devastation that a catastrophic illness can have on the family system.

Breast Cancer and Families

According to Compas et al. (1994), the diagnosis and treatment of cancer are sources of considerable psychological stress for patients and their families. Cancer is both an acute stressor, with its sudden onset and extreme stress reaction, and a chronic stressor, because the treatment effects may linger for years, and the fear of recurrence or death may never go away. Because of advances in detection and intervention technology, breast cancer is not a death sentence anymore – people can survive (Radina & Armer, 2001). Then again, if patients do not have access to this technology, they are likely to have more difficulties as the result of their cancer. According to Davey et al. (2005), although African American women have a 13% lower incidence of newly diagnosed breast cancer, they have a higher death rate, likely as a result of inadequate access to treatment.

Stressors

A breast cancer diagnosis poses a number of stressors and has many adverse effects on patients, partners, and family members.

The initial diagnosis is one of the biggest stressors in a patient's cancer journey, resulting in shock, surprise, sadness, fear, and – for some – hope (Weber & Solomon, 2010). The diagnosis also means the threat of death for some. Metastatic cancer (cancer that has spread from the original location to other parts of the body) represents a traumatic stressor that entails an ongoing, imminent life threat (Butler et al., 2005), which carries a two-year life expectancy on average and consequent increased physical and emotional symptoms such as depression, anxiety, and traumatic stress symptoms (Badr, Carmack, Kashy, Cristofanilli, & Revenson, 2010). Even if the prognosis is good, patients still face the loss of others parts of life such as functioning and appearance (Compas et al., 1994). Other difficulties include feelings of general distress, symptoms of post-traumatic stress (re-experiencing symptoms through nightmares and intrusive thoughts), avoidance symptoms (topic and person), and arousal symptoms such as irritability and sleep disturbances (Brown et al., 2007).

Once treatment has started, patients experience a wide range of additional stressors, including feeling alone, making treatment decisions (such as type of chemotherapy, or whether to have a lumpectomy vs a full, partial, or double mastectomy), receiving support, facing financial burden, waiting for test results, coming to terms with the diagnosis, dealing with bodily changes and changes to sexual intimacy, telling others about the diagnosis, integrating old and new identities, managing information needs, and distancing of individuals in their social network (Weber & Solomon, 2008; 2010). Side effects of treatment, such as secondary lymphedema of the arm (blockage in the transport of lymphatic fluid that results in a buildup of fluid and swelling, which makes the arm hard to move and bend, thus impeding daily life and household tasks) are stressful as well (Radina & Armer, 2001). The distress associated with these stressors can further reduce immune functioning, which can compromise treatment and recovery (Lebel, Rosberger, Edgar, & Devins, 2007); adjustment, however, can enhance the body's ability to repair itself (Weber & Solomon, 2010).

Stress continues in the post-treatment period, as breast cancer survivors face stressors such as physical and emotional disruptions, initiation of premature menopause, fears about recurrence (Mallinger, Griggs, & Shields, 2006), limitations in physical ability, and cancer-related problems with family or friends (Lebel et al., 2007). In regards to communication, Shields and Rousseau (2004) report that the end of active treatment can make it hard for women to talk about their cancer because family members do not want to upset the survivor by bringing it up, or enter into "denial mode," thinking that everything will be fine now. Finally, Lebel et al. (2007) describe the threat of cancer recurrence as the "sword of Damocles which hangs above the head of every cancer survivor" (p. 230), and thus, a continuous stressor. If the cancer comes back, families experience shock, grief, and altered expectations about recovery as they attempt to control symptoms, manage declines in functioning, minimize the patient's sense of isolation, and address existential issues about life and death (Sherman & Simonton, 2001).

In addition to directly affecting the patient, stressors associated with breast cancer affect partners and children as well. A cancer diagnosis ranks as one of the top sources of stress for partners, resulting in adverse effects on marital relationships and family functioning as well as psychological health (Compas et al., 1994). When the diagnosis is metastatic cancer, the partner faces the impending loss of a life partner and the difficult task of end-of-life conversations about issues such as hospice care and burial arrangements (Badr et al., 2010). Partners most at risk for traumatic stress reactions are those who have suffered recent and/or numerous family losses (Badr et al., 2010). In their study of male partners of women diagnosed with breast cancer, Hilton et al. (2000) observed a variety of reactions, including shock, disbelief, denial, anger, guilt, depression, anxiety, uncertainty, helplessness, fear, loss of control, and isolation. They noted a number of stressors as well, including physical care of the partner, treatment regimens, imposed changes in household tasks, and standing by and watching their partner suffer. Confusion from inaccurate or contradictory reports can amplify an already stressful situation, as can lack of treatment options, perceptions that the doctor is not spending adequate time with their partner, and the questioning of decisions by friends and family. Such feelings of distress can lead to lower marital satisfaction and lower family functioning.

The diagnosis can create relational stressors for couples as well. Skerrett (1998) states that couples are challenged to maintain a viable, balanced, mutual relationship while adjusting to the new roles of patient/caretaker, plus coping with uncertainties of separation and threatened loss. Resilient couples can achieve positive outcomes: The transformation in the relationship, which is part of adjustment, can give rise to new forms of communication, joint problem solving, and mutuality. Weber and Solomon (2008, 2010) identified several sources of dyadic stress, including concern about children, together time, and management of the treatment, as well as uncertainty regarding how to support one another, how to share the diagnosis with others, and how the disease will affect the relationship. At the family level, stressors include financial strain, family history (genetic inheritance and the need for genetic testing), being there for children, and worry on the part of family and children (Weber & Solomon, 2010).

Finally, children feel the effects of a cancer diagnosis. The extent to which children are affected depends on a number of factors, including their age and sex, and the sex of the affected parent (Badr et al., 2010); developmental stage and perceived ability to process disease-related information (Barnes, Kroll, Lee, Jones, & Stein, 1998); race or ethnicity (Davey et al., 2005); severity of treatment side effects; and the psychological health of the parents (Brown et al., 2007). Children whose mothers have breast cancer experience not only symptoms of anxiety and depression (Brown et al., 2007), but also distress, owing in part to the significant levels of stress in the household (Thatsum, Johansen, Gubba, Olesen, & Romer, 2008). In particular, school-aged daughters tend to have more difficulty with their mothers' diagnosis than sons (Brown et al., 2007). Children contend with stressors such as the disruption of family roles and routines, the risk of losing a parent to death, continued parental illness, changes in appearance, temporary loss of a parent through hospitalization and side effects, social stigmatization, caring for and comforting the parent, and changes in peer-group roles (Thatsum et al., 2008). The effects may be even stronger in adulthood. Fisher (2010) states that diagnosed women and their mothers or daughters share the transition psychologically, physically, and relationally as they take on new roles and responsibilities during the cancer journey.

Resources

Families have a number of coping resources at their disposal to help them through the cancer journey. In particular, social support and family communication are two of the most important resources families have to help them cope with breast cancer. First, a patient's partner is often the number one source of support throughout the ordeal. Kayser and colleagues (Kayser, Watson, & Andrade, 2007) identified three qualities that seemed to help couples navigate the process of dyadic coping: (a) relationship awareness (thinking about their relationship in the context of the illness), (b) authenticity (disclosing genuine feelings to their partners), and (c) mutuality (relating in a way that allows each partner to participate as fully as possible in the shared experience). In a study of breast cancer survivors, Weber and Solomon (2010) found that participants rated conversations with their partner about intrapersonal and identity issues as supportive and helpful in their coping process. Yet, giving support can itself become a source of stress for the partner (Badr et al., 2010), and many partners refuse to ask for help, particularly from the patient, which can leave the patient feeling frustrated. When partners do support one another and communicate effectively, they often see the marital relationship grow stronger and family coping improve (Hilton et al., 2000). Unsolicited or unhelpful advice, however, can become a source of stress unless the patient is receptive to the advice, and the advice is delivered optimistically and appropriately. In that case, such advice can become a significant coping resource for cancer patients and their families (Thompson & O'Hair, 2008).

Another important source of support emerges within the mother–daughter relationship. According to Fisher (2010), women who are diagnosed with cancer early in their lives often have mothers who are "there" for them in tangible, practical ways (which can sometimes be perceived as unhelpful or intrusive). Similarly, women who are diagnosed in later life have adult daughters who offer emotional support, although the mothers may worry about their daughters and how being there could affect them. Fisher found that when mothers or daughters of cancer patients listened without interruption or unsolicited advice, allowed the patients to vent, provided empathetic responses, showed humor, and displayed affection, the patients felt better adjusted and viewed the relationship as functioning adaptively. Emotional support and empathy from friends are helpful for both patients and their children as well, and they have been associated with fewer depressive symptoms in both mothers and children (Brown et al., 2007). Some other research suggests that adult children's ability to serve as sources of support is tied to how competently the patient communicates with them about her illness. Harzold and Sparks (2006) found that parents who communicated with openness, honesty, and a sense of humor helped their adult children serve as supporters in the cancer journey.

Finally, support from counseling professionals and other survivors via support groups is a critical coping resource for patients and their families. For instance, counseling professionals often offer interventions to families that enhance communication and emotional contact within the family, address illness-related changes in family structure, help families find meaning in illness, and manage mortality issues, greatly benefitting patients and their family members (Sherman & Simonton, 2001). Scott and associates (Scott, Halford, & Ward, 2004) compared how three different types of interventions (medication information, patient coping training, and a couple-coping training called CanCOPE) helped couples develop effective coping strategies, manage distress, and improve relational well-being. They found that the CanCOPE intervention produced large increases in how couples supported each other, decreased women's psychological distress and avoidance of negative thoughts, improved sexual intimacy with their partners, and altered perceptions of how their partners viewed them. Additionally, there are many community groups such as Bosom Buddies that are available to patients; unfortunately, there is a lack of community support for spouses (Dennis, Kunkel, & Keyton, 2008; Shields & Rousseau, 2004).

Second, in regard to communication, research has consistently shown that patients' ability to cope with breast cancer and emerge resilient is tied to the communicative support they receive in their family relationships (Fisher, 2010). In a summary of the communication research within the psycho-oncology literature, Beach and Anderson (2003) offer four conclusions about the role of communication in the cancer journey:

> (1) family members who communicate psychosocial support promote enduring family relationships, function as more effective caregivers, and experience less stress, (2) open, honest, and frequent communication is essential for ensuring that the wishes of patients and family members are heard and attended to when facilitating decision making regarding care options (although this is rare), (3) communication is associated directly with quality of care and life in terminal cancer, (4) throughout uncertain and often troubling cancer journeys, a vast amount of time and effort is invested by patients, family members, and health professionals as they attempt to manage understandings, relationships, and healing outcomes.
>
> (pp. 1–2)

Family communication also can decrease allostatic load (the physiologic costs of exposure to repeated stressors) and depressive symptoms, and increase compliance with treatment recommendations (Jones, Beach, & Jackson, 2004). Because of the link between communication and positive outcomes, counselors recommend interventions that help family members differentiate between adaptive and maladaptive communication patterns and coping efforts (Harris, Bowen, Badr, Hannon, Hay, & Sterba, 2009).

Whereas some studies suggest families communicate openly about cancer-related issues (Mallinger et al., 2006), other studies reveal that family members have a difficult time talking with one another about the cancer, either for fear of upsetting or burdening one another, or because they need to avoid thinking about the disease. As a result, family members tend to engage in protective buffering and avoid cancer-related topics. Parents often do this with their children by withholding information from them, despite the fact that the children often desire such information (Thatsum et al., 2008). When families avoid talking about the cancer, their individual and relational well-being can suffer. Shields and Rousseau (2004) state, "Avoidance of thinking or talking about the cancer experience disrupts patients' and spouses' abilities to communicate effectively and process the cancer experience cognitively and emotionally" (p. 98). In a study of cancer-related topic avoidance within married couples, Donovan-Kicken and Caughlin (2010) found that avoiding topics such as death, treatment, sexuality, being a burden, feelings, relating, and health care decreased patients' satisfaction with their relationships. In a study of 230 cancer survivors by Mallinger et al. (2006), women who reported any family avoidance had lower mental health scores than women who reported no family avoidance. Although the researchers did not claim that all open communication is good and topic avoidance is bad, they suggest that open communication works best in the context of positive communication skills such as validation and empathy. Indeed, effective self-disclosure about cancer topics can increase perceptions of intimacy in a relationship (Manne et al., 2004).

Coping Strategies and Outcomes

Numerous studies have examined how families cope when a loved one is diagnosed with breast cancer. Although most of the studies focus on the patient's coping efforts, some studies specifically examine dyadic coping efforts as (heterosexual) couples contend with breast cancer together. While fewer in number, other studies have also examined partners' and children's coping processes. Table 6.1 offers a number of the coping strategies identified in the literature.

Because avoidance strategies were difficult to identify, many cells in the bottom row of Table 6.1 remain blank, particularly at the social and communal levels. The placement of certain strategies also required some "thinking outside the schema," so to speak. For instance, research has shown that focusing on the benefits of the situation rather than the drawbacks (Kayser et al., 2007)

Table 6.1. A Sample of Coping Strategies Used as Families Face Breast Cancer.

		Problem-Focused	Emotion-Focused	Meaning-Focused	Relationship-Focused	Maintenance-Focused
Behavior	Individual	Find info.[2]	Yoga[3]	Normalization[3]	Give support to partner[3]	Show affection[1]
	Social	Mobilize one's support network[2]	Talk to women who have breast cancer[3]	Find meaning by educating others about cancer[3]	Support each other's coping efforts[4]	Visit with friends and family[3]
	Communal	Solve problems together[2]	Use humor with each other to ease tension[3]	Co-construct a sense of coherence[1]	Coordinate household responsibilities[4]	Keep family life going[2]
Cognition	Individual	Think of self as strong and capable[3]	Positive reframing[1]	Find benefits from one's experience[1]	Let the patient's coping style set the theme[1]	Understand issues with sexuality[1]
	Social	Get a second opinion[1]	Compare self to others with the illness[3]	Prayer[3]	Empathic coping[1]	See the experience as strengthening the relationship[1]
	Communal	Use family legacies for coping[2]	Talk about the future after treatment[1]	Jointly appraise cancer as a challenge[1]	Have a unified coping philosophy in the family[1]	Express solidarity to/with one another[1]
Avoidance	Individual	Minimize experience[3]	Keep busy in other activities[5]	Wishful thinking[5]	Hide true feelings from the patient[2]	Disengage from others in the family[4]
	Social	Maintain work relationships[3]	Keep busy with friends (outside the family)[5]		Titrate the what and when of partner comm. based on receptivity[1]	
	Communal		Family denial of the disease[4]		Agree to keep the cancer a secret from other members[2]	Mutual avoidance[4]

Source: 1 = Skerrett (1998); 2 = Hilton et al. (2000); 3 = Sullivan (1997); 4 = Kayser et al. (2007); 5 = Thastum et al., 2008

helps breast cancer patients and their families to cope. In a sense, those who cope in this manner are distancing themselves from the grim outlook that often accompanies breast cancer, and thus are avoiding the negative thinking that can consume patients and their families. Whereas this type of avoidance may be adaptive, because it allows optimism and hope, other types of avoidance – such as minimizing or denying the existence of the disease – are more maladaptive and can decrease relationship satisfaction (Donovan-Kicken & Caughlin, 2010) or impair coping (Shields & Rousseau, 2004).

At the individual level, appropriate expressions of fear, anger, and sadness, as well as efforts to confront problems, strengthen relationships, and find meaning, have all been identified as helpful strategies for women with diagnosed metastatic cancer (Austenfeld & Stanton, 2004). Repression of negative emotions and traumatic life experiences, on the other hand, have been linked to the development of breast cancer and reduced immune functioning (McKenna, Zevon, Corn, & Rounds, 1999). Likewise, negative dyadic coping efforts such as mutual avoidance and withdrawal have been associated with greater distress and decreased dyadic adjustment (Badr et al., 2010). In regard to communal coping, families who use positive appraisals can more easily make changes when a member is diagnosed with breast cancer than those who do not use positive appraisals (Radina & Armer, 2001). Patients and families with effective problem-solving skills tend to report lower levels of depression and anxiety, fewer cancer-related problems, and lower levels of distress as well (Nezu et al., 1999). Finally, Skerrett (1998) found that patients' and families' capacity to "go with the flow" and to modify and reprioritize their values are linked to greater mutual understanding, appreciation, and empathy within the family. She also cited a number of other factors associated with adaptation, such as having an identifiable, united coping philosophy; adjusting one's communication to the other family member's perceived level of reception; using multigenerational legacies as a way to craft current coping efforts; articulating beliefs regarding the origins of health and illness; and being able to control or influence the course of illness and well-being.

Case Study

For many patients and their families, a diagnosis of breast cancer is a pivotal turning point in their lives. When a patient is first diagnosed, feelings of stress, anxiety, anger, sadness, and worry are at their peak; but as treatment begins, these feelings can give way to optimism, hope, and positivity. The way families cope with these feelings and the resultant changes in the family system is critical in determining how well the family adjusts to the situation and whether it can emerge from a crisis more resilient than before. Countless books have been written to help cancer patients and their families cope: *Breast Cancer Survival Manual (4th edn): A Step-by-step Guide for the Woman with Newly Diagnosed Breast Cancer* by John Link (2000); *Chicken Soup for the Breast Cancer Survivor's Soul: Stories to Inspire, Support, and Heal* by Jack Canfield, Mark Hansen, and Mary Kelly (2006); *Breast Cancer Husband: How to Help Your Wife (and Yourself) During Diagnosis, Treatment, and Beyond* by Marc Silver (2004); and *The Hope Tree: Kids Talk About Breast Cancer* by Laura Numeroff, Wendy Harpham, and David McPhail (2001). There are also hundreds of websites dedicated to increasing breast cancer awareness and providing support for breast cancer patients and their families. One such website, *BreastCancerStories.org*, serves as the inspiration for the case study featured in this chapter. According to the website,

> BreastCancerStories.org gives Breast Cancer Patients and Care Givers access to virtual hugs and support from family members as well as other Patients and Care Givers across the globe going through a similar experience. Having just launched in the summer of 2006, more than 10,000 people log on every month to post and read stories about the trials of breast cancer and the triumphs of surviving the disease that claims the lives of far too many people every year.

With permission from Wendy McCoole, executive director and founder of the website, I created the following case using some of the experiences shared on the website to give "life" to the family portrayed in the case. I have changed names and places, as well as the exact wording of the stories, to help protect the confidentiality of the survivors. I also included some of my own experiences with cancer in the family to provide a first-hand account of a family member who had to cope with the negative effects that a cancer diagnosis can have on the family.

Case Overview

The Malone family has had a rough couple of years. In 2009, Linda Malone, age 50, was diagnosed with an aggressive form of breast cancer. Linda opted for a mastectomy and removal of nearby lymph nodes (some of which came back positive for malignancy), followed by chemotherapy and radiation. There is a possibility, however, that the treatments have not stopped the cancer. Because she is a realist, she is starting to come to terms with the possibility of losing this battle and what this will mean for her husband, Carl, and their three children. Her youngest child, Christopher, 13, is so busy with school and sports that he is rarely home; when he is home, he is in his room doing homework or playing on the computer. Leslie, a 21-year old junior studying nursing at a state university 150 miles away, drives home every other weekend to visit the family and help out around the house while Linda continues to recover. Jennifer, a 24-year-old newly-wed who lives across the country, constantly sends her mother articles about cancer treatments and alternative therapies that she finds on the web. Meanwhile, Carl has to figure out how to take care of Christopher, the household chores, and Linda while working 40-plus hours a week as a surgical nurse.

The bad news. Linda hit the snooze button for the third time. She desperately wanted to stay in bed but knew that, sooner or later, she would need to face the day. She finally turned off the alarm and staggered into the bathroom to start her shower. As she was reaching inside her medicine cabinet to get her razor and shaving cream, she glanced at the reminder card hanging on the door and noticed it was time to do her monthly breast self-exam. Because her mother had breast cancer, she knew this ritual was important; yet, she always wondered whether it was really effective. Regardless, she stepped inside the shower to allow the hot water to warm her chilly body. She lifted her left arm and began making little circles with her right hand around her breast. It was such a habit by now that she almost missed the tiny little bump next to her armpit. "Hmm. That's weird," she said, to no one in particular. It didn't hurt when she pressed it, but it didn't move either. "It's probably nothing," she thought to herself as she finished her shower. Nevertheless, she decided to call her doctor, given her family history. Upon hearing what she found and knowing how religiously she did her monthly self-exam, the nurse at the doctor's office scheduled her for an appointment to see the doctor that day. This was the last thing she needed. She hung up the phone, then dialed work to reschedule her meetings for the afternoon. She decided not to mention anything to her family for now so she wouldn't worry them. As she thought earlier, it's probably nothing.

From that day forward, Linda's life became a whirlwind of doctor appointments, tests, and answers. At her appointment, her doctor performed an ultrasound on the area, finding the lump to be "suspicious." Because Linda has fairly dense breasts, the doctor decided to send her to a clinic nearby that does digital mammography as it does a better job of differentiating a tumor from just thick breast tissue than traditional mammography. Within 48 hours of the test, her doctor called to say that the radiologist was worried and wanted her to schedule surgery to remove the lump, just to be safe. That was a Friday. On Monday, she met with a surgeon, and on Wednesday she had the lump removed – a procedure called a lumpectomy.

Two days later, she got the results she had been dreading: "I'm sorry to tell you this, but you have an aggressive type of invasive ductal carcinoma. We removed the tumor, but the margins weren't clear, which means we didn't get it all. You'll need to see a surgical oncologist to discuss a possible mastectomy and removal of lymph nodes in your armpit. After that, we have some options . . ."

The rest of the conversation was a blur. When she heard the word *cancer*, all she could think about was, "What am I going to tell the kids? How am I going to reschedule work to deal with all this crap?" Her mind then proceeded to play the "what if" game at lightning speed – What if they don't get it all? What if I have to do chemo and my hair falls out? What if it comes back (the cancer, not her hair)? What if I die? And it was at that point in the "what if" game that Linda started falling apart.

Thank goodness that Carl was sitting next to her in the doctor's office. When the doctor recommended the mammography, Linda decided to tell Carl about the lump so they could make a plan, just in case. They complemented each other quite well – whereas she tended to be emotional and was often more worried about other people than herself, Carl was a steady rock who would use his analytical and logical mind to tackle any problem ahead. So, the plan was for him to go with her to get any and all test results so he could take notes and ask questions in case Linda needed him. And boy, she needed him now, more than ever. When the appointment ended, and Linda had composed herself enough to leave, they walked out of the doctor's office hand-in-hand, a symbolic gesture that would come to represent this next phase in their lives.

Sharing the news. On the way home, Linda and Carl talked about how to tell the kids. They decided to be straightforward with the girls, because both were old enough to handle the news. The conversation with Jennifer was difficult, because she proceeded to question almost every decision they had made thus far: "What?! You're just telling me this now? Why didn't you tell me sooner?" "How do you know it is the aggressive type? Did you get a second opinion?" "Do you have to remove your whole breast? Can't they just go in there and get the rest of the cancer out?" Linda and Carl weren't surprised by her reaction, because Jennifer has a need to be in control of everything – including her mom's cancer. Although Linda didn't appreciate her daughter's attitude, she knew it was her way of coping with this difficult news.

The phone call with Leslie was difficult as well, but in a different way. Upon hearing the news, Leslie's first question was, "How are you doing with all this, Mom?"

Linda wanted to say, "I'm fine, honey, no need to worry about me," but instead, she was honest with her daughter. They had always been close and looked strikingly similar to each other. So she said, "I'm really scared, Leslie. Not so much about my prognosis, but about how I will look when all this is done. I don't want to be some scary, bald-headed, lopsided Cyclops-of-a-woman, but I know that the mastectomy and chemo, followed by radiation, are the best chances I have at beating this thing."

Leslie laughed and said, "With all those chemicals running through you, you may be able to shoot a powerful laser beam out of your remaining breast that can destroy anything in its path!" At first, Linda didn't get the reference, but then she remembered that Cyclops is a character on X-Men, one of her daughter's favorite comics. When she did get it, both women laughed loudly. The laughter soon turned to tears as the conversation continued.

The conversation with their son, Chris, was another matter. He was a typical teenager who spent most of his free time hanging out with friends and playing video games. Linda and Carl thought it would be a difficult conversation, but as usual, Chris surprised her. Linda came up with an idea on how to broach the subject with him. While surfing the internet, she came across a website called *cancergame.org* that contains a goofy video game developed by a college student, coping with cancer himself, for a class project. He later received some funding to put it online. She decided to use that game as a vehicle for talking with Chris about the disease.

When Chris came home from school, he found his Mom playing the game on the computer in the family room. "What's that?" he asked, trying not to look too interested in what his mom was doing.

"It's a video game I found on the Internet," she replied, adding "GOTCHA!" when she shot at a blob on the screen.

"But you never play games. What's so interesting about this one?"

"It's helping me to see that it is possible to beat cancer," she said, ending her session and turning towards her son.

"Oh, cancer? Is that why you've been kinda sad the past few days?"

"Yes, Chris. My doctor told me that I have cancer, and will have to have surgery and powerful drugs to help me fight this thing."

Chris thought for a second, and then said, "Can you show me how to play the game, too?"

For the next hour, Chris and his mom helped "T-cell," the character in the game, blast cancer cells to oblivion. They also talked about her disease and what he might expect over the next few months in regard to changes in her appearance and adjustments to the household duties.

After they finished playing, Chris gave his mom a hug, saying, "That was cool. Let's play again, OK?"

"OK, kid, but now it's time for your homework." And with that, Chris left the room, leaving Linda with a smile on her face that she didn't expect to have. She also felt hope for the first time since the start of the whirlwind that everything could turn out okay.

Changes and challenges. The first few weeks after the mastectomy were rough for Linda. She was sore, and she hated looking down and seeing . . . well . . . nothing on her left side except the sutures. She knew she shouldn't focus on what was missing, but she couldn't help feeling like she wasn't a whole woman anymore. She didn't even want Carl to see her naked, although he had to help her change the dressings on the sutures. Linda never thought of herself as a vain person, but all these changes left her wondering about the stranger looking back at her in the mirror. She definitely looked forward to getting the reconstructive surgery so she could feel whole again.

At least her genetic tests came back negative, so she could avoid having to decide whether or not to remove the other breast to prevent recurrence. Unfortunately, several of the lymph nodes that were removed during surgery tested positive for malignancy, which meant she had to face several weeks of chemotherapy followed by radiation treatment. From what she understood, the radiation would kill off any cancer cells that remained where the surgeon found the tumors, while the chemo would kill off any cancer cells that might have traveled outside the tumor locations.

Because chemo targets fast-dividing cells, the treatment would also kill other rapidly dividing healthy cells in the body, like her hair cells, meaning that she would likely lose her hair. Instead of waiting for the chemo to take her hair, she decided to take it herself, enlisting the help of her entire family in the process: Carl got the "honor" of shaving her head; Leslie picked out several nice head scarves for her to wear when it was warm outside; Chris found some cool hats for the winter; and Jennifer researched wig options, finding a great store in their area that worked with breast cancer survivors.

Meanwhile, Carl was doing his best to keep the house at least somewhat clean, cooking meals and taking care of both Linda and Chris. Thankfully, they had a large contingent of friends and family who brought over meals, ran errands, and gave Chris rides to his activities so Carl could remain at home with Linda. Leslie also came in every other weekend to help around the house and give Carl a much-needed break. Although he would do anything for Linda, Carl found himself feeling completely drained by the end of the week, finding any excuse to leave the house just to get some time for himself.

One morning while Linda was taking a nap, Carl decided to run to the local diner to get something to eat. While at the restaurant, he ran into a friend from work, who asked Carl to join him for lunch. Although he knew he should probably get back home, he decided to stay for a while, just to get caught up with the work gossip (he had been on leave for three weeks, and planned to return to work the following week). When his cell phone rang two hours later, he felt a pang of guilt when he saw that the call was from home. "Hello?" he said cautiously.

"What happened? Are you OK?" asked Linda, sounding genuinely worried.

"I'm fine. Sorry to worry you. I just stepped out to get some food. I'm on my way back."

"That sounds good," said Linda. "I'm glad you're OK. Bring me a burger and shake!" Carl hung up the phone, feeling even guiltier for not telling Linda the whole truth. Still, he didn't want Linda getting angry with him, and he had really enjoyed talking about something besides Linda's cancer. For a brief moment, he had almost felt normal again. He knew that the minute he walked through the door at home, he would be hit with the "new" normal that his life had become. With a sigh, he grabbed his food bag, said goodbye to his friend, and headed back to the house.

The three kids also found themselves facing changes in their lives throughout their mom's cancer journey. Right after Jennifer heard the news about her mother's diagnosis, she ran to the bathroom, took off her shirt, and proceeded with a 30-minute-long breast self-exam, which she repeated weekly for the next six months. She even had her doctor on speed dial so she could ask questions whenever she found anything remotely suspicious. She desperately tried to get off work to come home to visit, but couldn't because she had used so much of her vacation time for the wedding that she didn't have much time left. Jennifer also had little faith in the medical system; because she couldn't be there with her mom, she spent much of her free time surfing the Internet for information about alternative therapies that could help, much to her husband's chagrin.

Chris also spent a great deal of time on the Internet, but instead of looking for information, he was playing games with his friends or doing homework. In fact, his grades actually went up as a result of his new-found focus. Although he knew he should help out more, he spent as much time in his room as possible. Seeing his mother in pain and hearing her cry was more than he could take.

Instead of spending time on the computer or her studies, Leslie spent a good deal of time on the road traveling to and from home. She was exhausted all the time, and her course work was suffering as a result. Yet, dealing with her mother's cancer gave her a new goal in life – instead of being a surgical nurse like her dad, she decided to go into the oncology field so she could help families like her family cope with cancer. She wasn't going to be anything but a burden on her family if she didn't pass the semester.

Prognosis for the future. It has been eight months since the whirl-wind began. Linda is looking forward to having her entire family around her for Thanksgiving, not only because she loves seeing everyone, but also because she might know the results of her recent CT scan by then, and would need the love and support of everyone, depending on the results. Two weeks ago, she began feeling a consistent pain in her lower back. Because breast cancer can spread to the bones, she worried that all the surgeries, chemo, and radiation hadn't worked, and that it had metastasized after all. To see whether it had spread, her oncologist ordered a scan of her lower back and abdomen (in case it had spread to the liver, too). Typically, Linda has little tolerance for uncertainty, but this is one case where she prefers *not* knowing the results, because they could confirm what she already feels is the truth – she might not win this battle after all. As before, she hasn't told her kids about this latest development because she doesn't want to upset them if the test comes back negative. Unbeknown to her, however, Leslie shares a similar suspicion, and has already started going to grief counseling to help her cope with everything. She hasn't said anything about it to her family – not even to her mom – for fear of looking like she has given up hope. As for the other kids, Jennifer refuses to believe that her mom might die, and Chris hasn't even considered that a possibility. For now, Linda leans on Carl for support as she awaits the call from her doctor with the results.

Carl, too, leans on Linda for support, something he avoided doing early on in the journey, but not anymore. The incident at the diner was just the start of his hiding things from Linda. After two months of this, Linda confronted Carl, saying, "Why won't you talk to me anymore?"

"I do talk to you, all the time," said Carl, a little whinier than he wanted.

"Questions like 'What do you want for dinner?' and 'Are you in pain?' don't count. We used to talk about everything, and now it seems we talk about nothing but me."

Carl replied rather loudly, "But you're all that matters right now! What's going on with me is not important."

"It is to me!" shouted Linda, showing more anger and frustration than Carl had seen since the diagnosis. "This damn disease has taken away my body, my hair, and now my marriage. If you really want to know what's best for me, then you will snap out of this stupid 'poor Linda' mode and treat me like your wife, not your patient!"

Linda stormed out of the room, leaving Carl feeling a mix of embarrassment, frustration, and resentment – embarrassment because he knew she was right, frustration because he didn't know how else to act, and resentment because he was doing the best he could, given the circumstances.

Instead of letting her leave, Carl marched right after her, saying, "Fine! You want to know how I'm doing? Awful. Shitty. That damn disease has taken away my freedom *and* maybe even my best friend. I just want all this to be done with so we can live our lives again."

Rather than yelling back or retreating further, Linda stood there for a moment, and then started to laugh.

"What the hell are you laughing at?" he yelled, feeling more confused than ever before.

"I forgot how red your face gets when you're angry. You look like a cherry tomato!"

"Great. Glad you find this so amusing. Should we go and eat now?"

"Yep," she replied. "How 'bout a salad?" The two left the room together, arm-in-arm, feeling better than they had in a while.

Case Analysis

The Malone family is not unlike other families who have experienced breast cancer in regard to the stressors they experienced, the resources available to them, and how they coped with the situation. Although Linda describes herself as an emotional person, she enacted many problem-focused coping responses early on, including the proactive coping strategy of the regular breast self-exams and contacting the doctor's office, even in the face of doubt. Given this approach, it is no surprise that all three of her children are also problem-focused, although in different ways. Whereas Jennifer was focused on finding ways to help her mother, Chris was focused on what he could control – his schoolwork – and

Leslie was focused on helping her family. Linda also knew when to call upon her coping resources by telling her family about the cancer, and when to hold back under conditions of uncertainty so as to avoid worrying them. Indeed, her strong relationships with her husband and her daughter, Leslie, proved to be invaluable resources for her throughout the various stages of the journey.

Her family members, on the other hand, were more reluctant in turning to Linda for support. Instead of seeing the person on whom they had relied in the past, they saw Linda as a patient in need of care and support who should not be burdened with someone else's problems. In the case of her marriage, Carl's avoidance was a source of stress for Linda, resulting in their fight. This was an important turning point for the couple, because it allowed them to express what they were feeling to one another openly and honestly and regain the partnership that had been missing in the marriage.

Another important coping resource for the family was the Internet. It served not only as a good source of information for Jennifer as she conducted her research from afar, but also as a source of distraction for Chris as he attempted to get away from the reality of his mother's illness. It also gave Linda an interesting, effective, and non-threatening way for her to talk to Chris about the disease. There were examples of communal coping methods as well, such as the family's involvement in Linda's choice to shave her head before the chemo started, which allowed her to reframe one of her stressors (the change in her appearance) into an opportunity for the family to come together.

Questions for Further Analysis

1. Whereas Linda had supportive relationships with Carl and Leslie, she seemed to have a rather contentious relationship with her oldest daughter, Jennifer. Talk about that relationship and the implications it has for how both Linda and Jennifer handle the situation.
2. Refer back to the Family Adjustment and Adaptation Response model discussed in Chapter 2. In what phase is the Malone

family: adjustment or adaptation? If they are in the adjustment phase, assess how well they are doing. If they are in the adaptation phase, what prospects do they have for emerging from the crisis in a similar, if not better, state than before the crisis began?

3. Using the communication model presented in Chapter 4, analyze how communication affects and is affected by Linda's cancer diagnosis and treatment.

4. What does the future hold for this family if Linda's test shows that the cancer has metastasized to the spine and/or liver? How will they cope with this as a family and as individuals?

7

Stress and Coping during the Transition to Parenthood

For me, the first month was like a shock and awe campaign launched by an 8-lb. baby boy. Then one day he did stop crying when I picked him up. I learned how to nurse him laying down and we fell asleep together. Then he smiled. Then he followed my voice. Then he followed my face. Then he laughed and I thought where have you been? Why did we wait so long? And there it was, the magical bond. It grows more and more each day. Becoming a mother is by far the hardest thing I have ever done and it is the greatest thing I have ever done.

Kate, age 38 at the birth of her child.

Before children, much of the relationship is about negotiating how much time you spend together and on what mutual activities. With kids . . . it ends up being a scorecard with who did the most, whose turn it is, and whose non-baby activity is either most important (I have a meeting, so you need to leave work early to make it to daycare on time) or most deserved (I got up with him for three nights in a row, so I deserve to relax on the couch for 30 minutes).

Lynn, age 35 at the birth of her first child.

One of the primary tensions I'm experiencing right now is balancing being a mother and a professional. My partner and I have committed to raising our daughter at home rather than her being at a day-care or with someone other than us throughout the day. However, this is a real strain on my own responsibilities in both my parental and professional roles . . . The result is that I feel guilty. I feel guilty if I leave the house on Sundays because then there is little-to-no time together with the three of us. I feel guilty if I do work when I'm at home with the baby because I'm there to take care of and interact with her. Perhaps it's my strict Catholic background that induces all of this guilt, but whatever it is, I spend much of my time feeling guilty.

Emily, age 33 at the birth of her child.

The transition to parenthood is a significant event in the family lifecycle. Every year, there are approximately 6 million pregnancies in the United States, more than 4 million of which end up in live births (American Pregnancy Association, n.d.). Whereas 60% of these births are to couples, many children in the US today are born to single mothers, same-sex parents, unmarried cohabitating parents, or live with adoptive parents (Smock & Greenland, 2010). Whether through birth, adoption, or marriage, the transition to parenthood marks a major change in the family system that can often lead to drastic changes in relationship experiences for two-parent families (Doss, Rhoades, Stanley, & Markman, 2009) and single-parent families alike (Copeland & Harbaugh, 2010). As family therapist Betty Carter claims, "Once there is a child, life will never be the same, for better or for worse" (Carter, 1999, p. 249).

There is much debate in the literature as to how the transition to parenthood affects new parents. On the one hand, researchers and new parents alike can outline the many difficulties that arise from having a baby. The quotes that you read at the start of the chapter from Emily and Lynn – two mothers who have experienced this transition – highlight some of the difficulties new parents face. On the other hand, new parents experience many benefits as the result of the addition to the family. Kate's quote focuses on the benefits of parenthood as seen through the growth and accomplishments of her child. The question remains, what makes the transition to parenthood a crisis for some and not others?

Instead of arguing whether or not the transition to parenthood is problematic, this chapter explores the factors, stressors, resources, and coping strategies that differentiate successful families from those that are less successful in making the transition to parenthood. As with the other case study chapters, page limitations prevent a complete review of the literature, given the extensive number of studies on the transition to parenthood. Instead, the focus is on the stressors, factors, and strategies that have received the greatest amount of attention. You will first read about the risk factors and stressors that families experience during the transition to parenthood, followed by a discussion of the protective factors and the resources available to families during this period. Then, you will read about the coping strategies that new parents use to adjust to their new life circumstance. Throughout the discussion, you will see that family communication plays a critical role in family adaptation and adjustment before, during, and after the addition of a new child. The chapter concludes with a case study of a family that experienced the transition to parenthood. It is based on the lived experiences of friends, family, and colleagues who have gone through this developmental stressor, as well as my own experience as a first-time parent.

The Experiences of New Parents

From a life course perspective, "Parenthood is a normal life event in which the birth of a baby temporarily upsets the internal structure of the family system as boundaries, roles, and tasks are reorganized to accommodate the new member" (Ventura & Boss, 1983, p. 867). Indeed, the arrival of a first child marks a significant transition in the life of new parents, during which they must negotiate personal, familial, social, and often professional change (Levy-Shiff, Dimitrovsky, Chulman, & Har-Even, 1998). For some new parents, the change results in significant stress. LeMasters (1957) was one of the first scholars to write about the transition to parenthood, describing this period as a crisis in which families face extreme disorganization. Other researchers have followed suit, finding that new parents report an increase in personal stress after the birth of a baby (Miller & Sollie, 1980). This stress is exacerbated when other negative life events happen at the same time, such as job loss or the death of a family member (Mercer & Ferketich, 1990).

Mothers may have a particularly difficult time during the

transition to parenthood because they are often the primary care-givers of the children and experience a great deal of role strain as they attempt to balance a new child with their other duties inside and outside the house. According to Pinquart and Teubert (2010), whereas the birth of a child "may be associated with positive experiences, such as watching children grow," it is also associated with negative experiences "for mothers in particular . . . such as decline in the quality of the couple relationship, physical exhaustion, increase in psychological distress, and difficulties with developing effective parenting behaviors" (p. 316). Depression is a major concern as well, with 13% to 27% of new mothers showing some symptoms of depression after the birth of a baby. Fathers have trouble, too, and have showed signs of increased stress and depression after the birth of their first baby (Castle, Slade, Barranco-Wadlow, & Rogers, 2008).

The couple's relationship can also suffer as a result of the transition to parenthood. A number of studies have identified declines in relationship satisfaction after the birth of a baby (e.g., Doss et al., 2009; Mitnick, Heyman, & Smith Slep, 2009). Whereas Stamp and Banski (1992) attribute such effects to an overall decrease in relational communication after the birth of a child, Kluwer and Johnson (2007) found that it was an increase in the number of conflicts that led to declines in relational quality. They qualified this result, however, by blaming post-birth declines in relationship satisfaction on problems that existed during pregnancy rather than the transition to parenthood; yet, the transition likely intensified the problems that already existed.

For other new parents, the benefits of the situation outweigh any short-term stress that results from the change. Researchers suggest that the short-term negative effects brought about by worry regarding the delivery and subsequent lack of sleep and changes in routine after the birth eventually go away (Castle et al., 2008). Keizer and associates (Keizer, Dykstra, & Poortman, 2010) found that the transition to parenthood does not affect women's life satisfaction, loneliness, or positive affect, and tends to decrease negative affect. Becoming a dad did not significantly impact life satisfaction or negative affect for men, either. In regard to relationship satisfaction, some studies show that the transition to parenthood has little effect on marital well-being, particularly when new parents are compared with childless couples (Mitnick et al., 2009), and that it could even increase perceptions of satisfaction and commitment for some couples (Doss et al., 2009).

Stressors

Research on the transition to parenthood has typically focused on heterosexual, married couples who conceive a child naturally, then deliver the child when he or she is full-term. Yet, complications can arise at several points along this process that can add to any stress the couple is already experiencing as they make room for a new member of the family. These range from infertility issues that prevent a couple from conceiving a child without outside intervention to threatened or actual miscarriage of the pregnancy to premature birth. This period is particularly difficult when the child is born with special needs, or when there are multiple births (twins, triplets). The transition to parenthood for families who adopt a child, particularly through international adoption, contains its own set of stressors ranging from getting health information about the biological parents to wondering what to tell the child about his or her adoption, as well as how to teach a child from another country or ethnicity about his or her native culture. Single-parent households, same-sex couples, unmarried couples, and grandparents who raise their grandchildren all face similar stressors as they make the transition to parenthood, but also unique stressors that pertain to their situation as falling outside the traditional trajectory of family life.

A number of parental, child, and relational characteristics influence the transition to parenthood. Smock and Greenland (2010) identify several issues at the parental level, such as (a) an increased age at marriage, which can lead to delayed childbearing and fertility issues (but also more maturity and financial stability, which can aid in infant development); (b) the extent to which the pregnancy is planned or unplanned, with unplanned pregnancy being associated with more negative outcomes; and (c) education level, with higher maternal education associated with better infant development. They also cite race, ethnicity, social class, and the rise of "multiple partner fertility" (having biological children with more than one partner) as playing a role in the transition to parenthood. Another factor is infertility, which can be a significant source of stress during the pre-pregnancy period and can lead to distance between an infertile couple and their support network (Gameiro, Boivin, Canavarro, Mauda-Ramos, & Soares, 2010). According to Carter (1999), "The intensity of the negative experiences of infertility is often overlooked by the couple's family, friends, or even therapist, and there is a danger that the couple will identify themselves as damaged or stigmatized . . . creating stress, depression, and paralysis" (p. 259). Doss et al. (2009) note that new parents' views of conflict in their own parents' marriage could also influence their transition to parenthood. They found that mothers whose parents experienced higher levels of conflict and divorce experienced greater declines in relationship satisfaction after the birth of their own children. Maternal depression and pregnancy risk affect the transition to parenthood as well (Mercer & Ferketich, 1990), as do emotional instability, an insecure attachment style, psychological disorders, impulsiveness, a need for more autonomy (Mitnick, et al., 2009), and poverty and homelessness (Carter, 1999).

Another critical factor is the expectations that parents-to-be have about parenthood. If parenthood fails to live up to expectations, then new parents could experience more difficulty throughout the transition (Levy-Shiff, Goldshmidt, & Har-Even, 1991). As Stamp (1994) states, "The preparation for parenthood is particularly difficult. Regardless of expectations or preparation, one cannot know fully what is entailed; yet, one acts upon the knowledge one has to try and predict what parenthood will entail" (p. 94). For example, even though new parents understand that caring for a child requires sacrifices, many new parents cite the loss of autonomy, concerns about caring for the baby (such as the first illness), a sense of obligation, and resentment over traditional roles as mother and wife as significant problems related to their adjustment to parenthood (Odom & Chandler, 1990; Splonskowski

& Twiss, 1995; Stamp & Banski, 1992). One sometimes over-whelming expectation placed on new mothers is breastfeeding their infants. According to Purdy (2010), breastfeeding may not be instinctive, effortless, or natural for all women, especially in the current US culture, where formula is pushed and the breast sexualized, and where fear of disfigurement, negative community reaction to breastfeeding in public, and the personal inconvenience of pumping at work because of inflexible maternity leave policies all militate against the practice. At the same time, some women feel extreme pressure to breastfeed their child. Thus, breastfeeding is a big stressor for new moms.

At the child level, a number of factors influence new parents' transition to parenthood. Loutzenhiser and Sevigny (2008) report that infants typically wake every three to four hours for the first three months, then settle into longer patterns of night sleeping thereafter. When children have trouble sleeping, however, stress increases, particularly for the parent who works outside the home, because the primary caregiver who is home with the infant can sleep when the child sleeps. Keefe and colleagues (Keefe, Karlsen, Lobo, Kotzer, & Dudley 2006) and McKay and associates (McKay, Ross, & Goldberg, 2010) also identified colic or inconsolable crying for long periods of time as significant concerns among new parents. These crying episodes can last three to four hours and can continue until the child is four to six months old. Additionally, Odom and Chandler (1990) note that premature births result in having "technologically assisted infants" (infants who need some form of technology to survive and thrive), which can cause different stressors than full-term births, particularly when the baby needs special attention after coming home. Even the sex of the child has been found to influence the transition to parenthood, with Doss et al. (2009) finding that mothers who give birth to girls reported larger drops in marital satisfaction than did those who gave birth to a boy, likely because the fathers are less active in caring for girls than for boys. Finally, Levy-Shiff et al. (1991) found that the processes underlying the transition to parenthood in adoptive and biological families differ, because adoptive parents confront unique challenges, stresses, and conflicts different from those of biological parenthood. They state, "Adoptive parents are [often] infertile couples who attain adoption after long years of stress, painful disappointments, and narcissistic injuries related to intrusive medical treatments and to their inability to have children" (p. 131).

At the relational level, Shapiro and Gottman (2005) note that the presence of destructive marital conflict has been linked to attentional and emotion regulation difficulties and psychological problems in children. As such, how a couple manages conflict is an important indication of family functioning during the transition to parenthood. Another factor may be the frequent moves associated with military life. Although Splonskowski and Twiss (1995) hypothesized that the mobile life of military families may make the transition harder on military mothers, they found little difference between civilian and military moms; it should be noted, however, that they did not account for whether the transition occurs during peace or wartime, which would likely influence the transition. Other relational factors include the timing of the child after marriage, with longer marriage before birth predicting smaller decreases in marital satisfaction; and premarital cohabitation, with fathers reporting larger sudden decreases in relationship dedication and increased negative communication after the birth (Doss et al., 2009).

Among the biggest sources of stress that new parents face at the relational level are role strain and household division of labor (Stamp, 1994). According to Copeland and Harbaugh (2010), the roles new parents acquire upon the birth of their baby may result in role strain, which can increase their vulnerability and stress response. Despite the fact that many new parents also have careers, research on heterosexual married couples has shown that the lion's share of household labor remains on the woman's shoulders. Huston and Holmes (2004) report that the transition to parenthood results in an expansion of work at home, with the number of tasks for new mothers increasing from 3.9 to 28 tasks per day; new fathers, however, only go from 1.9 to 8.3 tasks per day. For dual-income families, childcare in the United States is a top practical concern when couples become parents, given that the

US is the only industrialized nation in the world that leaves it to the individual families to arrange and pay for childcare. Because work and family are the primary spheres of activity for most individuals, redefining family roles is a central developmental task of the transition to parenthood, and the results can have far-reaching effects for the individual, the family, and society (Golden, 2001).

Resources

After reading the preceding section, it may seem that new parents are doomed to a life of stress and difficulty during the transition to parenthood. Yet, there are a number of protective factors and resources that help ease new parents through this life-changing time. At the individual level, parents who have high self-esteem and a sense of control or mastery over their lives make the transition to parenthood more easily, particularly in regard to acquiring new skills to care for the infant or preventing postpartum depression (Copeland & Harbaugh, 2010; Mercer & Ferketich, 1990). Levy-Shiff et al. (1991) identified a number of predictors that determined how new parents survive the transition to parenthood, including ego-strength for the biological parents, and feelings of deprivation, social support, and self-concept for the adoptive parents. They found that the sturdier the biological parents' ego-strength and the higher their expectations regarding familial experiences pre-birth, the more positive their postnatal familial experiences were. For adoptive families, the more support they received and the higher their expectations, the more satisfactory familial experiences they reported after the arrival of the baby.

At the family/dyadic level, Tomlinson and Irwin (1993) found that having an average or happy family of origin, and having similar views concerning traditional sex-role expectations, interests, ideals, goals, and backgrounds, helped new parents in their transition to parenthood. For couples, having a strong, supportive relationship before the birth is another critical protective factor as they make the transition. Indeed, having a supportive, loving husband during pre-pregnancy is key to an increase in marital satisfaction for women after the birth of the baby (Shapiro & Gottman, 2005). Curan and colleagues (Curan, Hazen, Jacobvitz, & Feldman, 2005) believe relationship maintenance is critical to sustaining marital satisfaction and juggling roles during the transition to parenthood, and sought to identify predictors of couples' maintenance during this time. Their study highlights new parents' emotional attachment to their own parents and mental representations of those parents' marital relationships as key predictors, finding that new parents with rich memories of their own parents' marriage scored higher on maintenance than those with less rich memories. They also found that new parents with a dismissing attachment style (those who have a difficult time trusting others and are more self-reliant) had a lower level of maintenance and less rich recollection of their parents' marriage than those who are secure (trusting of others and optimistic about relationships) or preoccupied (fearful of rejection but with a great need to be in relationships). Parental communication is an important coping resource as well: couples who communicate effectively and are highly committed to the parenting role work together to maintain family integrity, and thus minimize the negative effects of the transition (Ventura & Boss, 1983).

Finally, at the social level, support from one's social network is a critical coping resource for families who make the transition to parenthood. Research points to the importance of both perceived and received social support in reducing parental distress for single and married new parents (Copeland & Harbaugh, 2010), as well as biological (Castle et al., 2008) and adoptive families (Levy-Shiff et al., 1991). Immediate family members provide a great deal of support during the transition period (Gameiro et al., 2010). In particular, Dun (2010) highlights the bond between new parents and grandparents as an important relationship during the transition to parenthood. In an interview with new parents, he found that communication resulted in both positive moments (such as announcing the pregnancy) and negative moments (such as being critical or overprotecting) in the parent/grandparent relationship during the transition to parenthood. Despite its importance, some research suggests that social support drops over time as the new parents steadily develop new routines and adjust to life with their new baby (Castle et al., 2008).

Another important coping resource is the variety of childcare and birthing classes offered at hospitals, doctors' offices, and community centers. Researchers generally find that interventions focused on enhancing family relationships can have a significant and substantial positive impact on parents' and children's well-being. In a meta-analysis of 142 studies, for example, Pinquart and Teubert (2010) found that parents who attended a class showed more positive parenting, lower levels of parenting stress, less child abuse or neglect, and more behaviors targeted at promoting child health than those who did not receive such an intervention. Other researchers have tested the effectiveness of specific programs. Keefe et al. (2006) examined the effectiveness of the "REST" program [R(eassurance) E(mpathy) S(upport) T(ime-out)], where nurses visit new parents' homes to help them with irritable infants. Families that had home visits from REST nurses experienced significantly less parenting stress related to parent–child interaction than those that did not. Similarly, Shapiro and Gottman (2005) created the "Bringing Baby Home Workshop," a two-day psycho-communicative-educational workshop for transition-to-parenthood couples. The workshop used lectures, role playing, and exercises to teach new parents skills for coping with conflict, maintenance, and parenting. They found that relationship quality stayed relatively stable in the workshop group, but declined in the control group of couples who did not attend the workshop. The researchers blamed the short-term dip in marital quality right after the birth of the baby to an increase in marital conflict that occurred because of the workshop, where they were taught to be open and honest with each other about their needs. The skills that workshop attendees learned, however, helped them overcome the dip in the long run.

Coping Strategies and Outcomes

Given the difficulties documented in the literature, it is not surprising that researchers have identified a number of coping strategies individuals and couples use to deal with the transition to parenthood. Whereas many of the studies have focused primarily on the mother's individual and social coping efforts, a number of more recent studies have included the father as well, allowing researchers to identify the couple's communal coping efforts as they work together to negotiate household labor and childcare duties. As with the previous chapters, sample strategies have been classified using the coping matrix introduced in Chapter 4 (see Table 4.1). The two blank cells in the Communal Coping/Avoidance strategy row reflect the difficulty of finding meaning-focused or relationship-focused communal avoidance strategies in the literature. A likely reason for this gap is that a new baby is not easily avoided; as such, much of the research on communal coping has focused on active-cognitive and active-behavioral strategies that the new parents use, rather than avoidance strategies the couple employs together away from the baby.

In regard to coping effectiveness, Levy-Shiff et al. (1998) found that a mother's active, problem-focused coping efforts increased with time and were effective at decreasing maternal stress and increasing infant involvement and efficacy. Emotion-focused coping remained relatively stable across the transition to parenthood, but was associated with increased maternal distress and decreased involvement in caregiving and affiliative behaviors. O'Brien and associates (O'Brien, Buikstra, Fallon, & Hegney, 2009) found that women who breastfed for longer durations used various coping strategies to help them manage the challenges of early motherhood, such as increasing breastfeeding knowledge, purposefully relaxing (using such techniques as deep breathing, progressive muscle relaxation, or visualization), looking after themselves, using positive self-talk, challenging unhelpful beliefs, engaging in active problem solving, setting short- and long-term goals, and practicing mindfulness (staying in the moment). At the dyadic level, Ventura and Boss (1983) found that doing things with children, being a parent, investing in children, maintaining family stability, trusting one's partner, and being thankful were the most helpful strategies for new parents. Crying, reliving the past, watching TV, wishing the baby wasn't there, believing life would be better without the baby, taking advantage of economic benefits, and shopping with friends were least helpful. Levy-Shiff et al. (1991) found that the more adoptive parents used emotional distancing and denial as coping mechanisms, the more satisfying experiences they reported. Finally, Ahlborg and Strandmark (2006) studied the quality of intimate relationships of 535 Swedish first-time parents six months post-delivery. They found that couples who had realistic expectations; shared responsibility; provided mutual support and encouragement; had mutual respect and regard; shared common goals and values; shared experiences emotionally, sensually, and sexually; broke the daily routines; had regular talks about different matters and were able to listen to one another; solved problems collaboratively; shared wakeful nights; and sought support from social networks had the best chance for adjusting to the transition to parenthood.

Case Study

Many popular movies and shows like *Parenthood*, *Father of the Bride II*, *Nine Months*, *Look Who's Talking*, and *Three Men and a Baby* capture the absurd and sometimes comedic life with children. Other shows such as *Super Nanny* and *Nanny 911*, and books like *What to Expect when You're Expecting* by Heidi Murkoff and Sharen Mazel (2008), *What to Expect the First Year* by Heidi Morkoff, Arlene Eisenberg, and Sandee Hathaway (2009), *The Girlfriend's Guide to Surviving the First Year of Motherhood* by Vicki Iovine (1997), and *The New Father* by Armin A. Brott (2004), offer suggestions for how to cope with the ups and downs of parenthood from pregnancy throughout childhood. But there is nothing more informative about the transition to parenthood than reading stories from individuals who have survived this process. Thus, I based the case in this chapter on stories from my friends, family, and colleagues who have had children and lived to tell about it. I, too, am the mother of a young child, and can easily relate to many of the studies identified in this chapter that outline the difficulties associated with parenthood.

Table 7.1. A Sample of Coping Strategies Used During the Transition to Parenthood.

		Problem-Focused	Emotion-Focused	Meaning-Focused	Relationship-Focused	Maintenance-Focused
Behavior	*Individual*	Learn new skills[1]	Watch TV[1]	Focus on the benefits[1]	Pick up household duties[6]	Play with baby[1]
	Social	Seek support from work for childcare[2]	Seek counseling[6]	Think about what parents went through[2]	Support the partner's parenting role[5]	Celebrate with grandparents[9]
	Communal	Go to classes with partner[10]	Share feelings[3]	Talk about expectations[5]	Coordinate schedules[2]	Maintain family stability[1]
Cognition	*Individual*	Adjust expectations[5]	Look to the future[1]	Positive self-talk[8]	Trust one's partner[1]	Think about how important partner is[7]
	Social	Get ideas from friends and family[1]	Seek friends who understand[1]	Turn to one's faith[1]	Mutual listening[7]	Focus on how the baby brings couple closer together[7]
	Communal	Talk through alternative solutions[7]	Share fantasies of a future[7]	Have shared meaning for arrangements[2]	Consider each other's needs[6]	Have mutual respect/regard[7]
Avoidance	*Individual*	Distance from problems[4]	Wish baby wasn't here[1]	Deny probs. with infertility[4]	Fulfill one's own needs (not partner/baby)[8]	Get some alone time[8]
	Social	Get away with friends[3]	Shop with friends[1]	Downplay past social life[5]	Judge what is important in a situation[7]	Have outside friendships[1]
	Communal	Withdraw from friends[11]	Look ahead as a couple to when the baby's older[7]			Have a date night away from baby[6]

Source: 1 = Ventura & Boss (1983); 2 = Golden (2001); 3 = Miller & Sollie (1980); 4 = Levi-Shiff et al. (1991); 5 = Stamp (1994); 6 = Tomlinson & Irwin (1993); 7 = Ahlborg & Strandmark (2006); 8 = O'Brien et al. (2009); 9 = Dun (2010); 10 = Splonskowski & Twiss (1995); 11 = Gameiro et al. (2010)

Case Overview

John Smith, 35, and Patty Johnson-Smith, 37, have been married for five years. Instead of getting married and having children in their twenties, as is typical for many couples, they decided to wait to start a family after establishing their careers – John as a high-school English teacher and debate coach, and Patty as a marketing communication executive. They are just about to celebrate their daughter, Chelsea's, first birthday. John and Patty had a strong relationship going into the pregnancy, often traveling, sleeping in late, and having quality alone time on the weekends. They knew it was going to be difficult, but felt that they had the financial and social support resources around them to help them through the first year. And the timing was perfect. Because Chelsea was born at the start of the summer, John was able to stay at home without taking paternity leave; unfortunately, Patty was only able to take 6 weeks of maternity leave before returning full-time to her job. Although they had read all the books, taken every parenting class they could find, and talked with other couples who had children, they still were not prepared for the changes they experienced when Chelsea was born.

Pregnancy. Patty stared at the stopwatch; 1 minute and 35 seconds had passed. Only another minute and a half to wait. She had been through this seven times before – waking up in the morning, running to the bathroom, and trying to pee on a stick (without peeing on her hand) so she could find out if she was pregnant or not. The first time they started trying, the test came back positive, but she had her period a week later, indicating that she had an early miscarriage. The next six times, the test came back negative. She was getting tired of the disappointment, holding out little hope that this time would be any different. She regretted waiting until her 30s to start having a family. She thought it would be easy to get pregnant – heck, it seemed like every time her mother had sex, she had a baby! Instead, Patty and John struggled with trying to get pregnant. Her doctor told her to give it a year and then they would try fertility treatment.

Here they were, eight months of playing "soccer without a goalie" and still no score.

When the stopwatch reached 3 minutes, she sighed, walked over to the bathroom countertop, and picked up the pregnancy test. She clearly saw one line, but then she thought she saw another line. It was very faint, but nevertheless present. She re-read the directions; they clearly said that even a faint second line meant that the pregnancy hormone was present. She had a hard time believing what she was seeing, and decided to retake the test the next morning before saying anything to John. When she repeated the test the next day, the second line was still there – and even a little brighter! With a smile, she ran and got her phone, snapped a shot of the test, and sent it to John with the message, "GOOOOOOOOOOOOOAL!"

The next eight months seemed to fly by as Patty and John prepared for the baby. First, they waited until the end of the first trimester to tell anyone, given that they had miscarried once before. During that time, they read every pregnancy book they could find to make sure Patty was eating all the right foods, doing all the right exercises, and taking all the right vitamins. Patty seemed to spend a lot of that time in the bathroom because of the morning sickness she was experiencing. They also wanted to find the perfect way to tell their families, and decided to give both sets of grandparents-to-be a framed "photo" of the baby – the 12-week ultrasound picture. Although they got to see the reaction of John's family, because they live just 30 minutes away, they had to settle for hearing the reaction of Patty's family, who live 500 miles away, on the telephone.

The second trimester also flew by, marked by the many classes that Patty and John took to prepare for the birth. Together, they completed a basic childbirth class, a child safety class, a child-care class, and a breastfeeding class. John attended a "Bootcamp for New Dads" that was run by dads, for dads, with no moms allowed. John was amazed to see the "old timers" who ran the class come in with their kids; one dad even had triplets with him! The highlight of the second part of the pregnancy was finding out the sex of the baby during the 18-week anatomy ultrasound. It was a girl! They even had a name already picked out – Chelsea. Patty was thrilled, but John was a little nervous, because he had no idea how to take care of a little girl. Yet, the class John took helped him to relax a bit and look forward to having a little girl.

The "birth" day. As Patty's due date approached, John and Patty spent time setting up the nursery so everything would be ready for the baby's arrival. By this point, Patty couldn't do very much, weighing 30 pounds more than she had at the start of the pregnancy and feeling very wobbly. John didn't mind doing the extra work, because it gave him something to do. They also enjoyed going to the baby showers their friends, family, and colleagues threw for them. They were amazed at their loved ones' generosity and felt lucky to have such a tight-knit group supporting them. Finally, they created a birth-plan that orchestrated everything that would happen at the time of delivery, ranging from the music that would be played to the circumstances under which Patty would get an epidural. (The plan was to do a "natural" childbirth, unless the pain got so severe that she would need a pain block to finish the delivery.) Everything seemed to be going perfectly, until the big day arrived. Then, things started spiraling out of control.

First, the baby's heart rate was irregular, and went down every time a contraction came. Despite pushing, the baby wouldn't come out, so the doctor decided to do an emergency c-section for the sake of the baby. Although Patty and John had considered that possibility, the reality of it was different, forcing them to abandon the fantasy of an easy delivery and recovery, and face the prospect of a prolonged and painful healing process after the birth.

Second, despite all of their pre-birth conversations about co-parenting and sharing equally in Chelsea's care, Patty began to realize that John might not live up to his end of the bargain. Because the nurses felt it was important for new parents to bond with the baby, Chelsea spent a lot of time in the room, and Patty spent a lot of time wincing in pain every time Chelsea started to cry. During the second night, as John once again slept through Chelsea's cries, Patty got up out of bed, shook John, and said "I have just had my stomach cut open and I'm in a lot of pain. Get your behind up and help me with the baby. Wake up and welcome to parenthood!"

Feeling groggy, John replied, "You are standing over me looking *really* scary."

Patty said, "Yes, and I'm prepared to do whatever it takes. Get up." Whether that was the medicine speaking, or exhaustion, that interaction seemed to set the tone for the next six months.

The final problem came when, by the fourth day in the hospital, Patty's milk still hadn't come in. According to all the books they had read, she should have started producing milk around the third or fourth day. Instead, the baby was losing weight as opposed to gaining weight, which worried Patty and John, although it didn't concern the doctor, because a small amount of weight loss is normal until the mother's milk comes in. To add insult to injury, she had a difficult time getting Chelsea to "latch" or drink properly from her breast. It was embarrassing to have total strangers poke and prod at her breast to help her and the baby learn the process of breastfeeding, which should have come naturally, but didn't.

After another unsuccessful feeding, Patty turned to John and said, "If things don't turn around soon, I think we should start supplementing with formula."

John said, "You know how important it is to breastfeed in the first few months. Keep trying and you'll be fine."

"Easy for you to say," uttered Patty under her breath. She resented the pressure from him and others in the hospital to keep breastfeeding, but she knew they were right. Then, she turned to look at her beautiful baby girl who was quietly snoozing on her chest, smiled, closed her eyes, and joined her daughter in slumber.

The first six months. The day finally came when Patty and John got to take Chelsea home. Patty was still sore, but doing better than she expected as she crawled gingerly into the back seat of the car to sit next to the baby. Patty hoped that the sleeping arrangements they had made at home for Chelsea would make the late night feedings easier and reduce some of the problems they had at the hospital. They had a crib set up for the baby in the nursery, and a bassinet in Patty and John's room, complete with vibrating mattress and night light, to help Chelsea sleep. They also had a co-sleeper attachment on their bed so that when Chelsea woke to eat, all Patty had to do was roll over and they could both remain lying down. Chelsea had her own idea, however: the only place she would sleep that first night at home was in Patty's arms, lights on. The next morning, Patty walked downstairs, disheveled, looking as if she'd been partying hard all night.

Her mom, who was spending two weeks at the house to help out, looked at her and asked, "How are you doing?"

"Overwhelmed," said Patty, before collapsing and weeping into her mother's arms.

It didn't help when John, looking fairly well rested, came downstairs carrying Chelsea and saying, "Patty, Chelsea's hungry again. Could you feed her while I take a shower?"

Patty took Chelsea into her arms, glared at John, and walked back upstairs to nurse the baby in her bedroom.

With time, the family started to fall into a routine. Patty and John also discovered that Chelsea could drink milk just as easily from a bottle as she could from the breast, which meant that John could do night time feedings. But just when Patty and John were thinking things were going well, Chelsea started crying for hours at a time. John and Patty would take turns walking Chelsea around the house at all hours of the night, trying to calm her down. They tried wrapping her tightly in a baby blanket, but Chelsea would wiggle her way out of the swaddling. They bounced her, rocked her, and sang to her, but nothing seemed to work.

Around that time, Patty began to seriously doubt her parenting abilities, thinking to herself, "If I'm doing this right, why is she still crying?" She also secretly wondered when the magical bond would form that would make all of these problems seem insignificant. She couldn't talk to her mother or John about these feelings; she was ashamed. Then one day, her Aunt Rose called and all her worries came pouring out. "How do people do this? Why do they do it again? Will she ever stop crying?"

Her aunt listened, then said, "Patty, family takes time."

Although she couldn't appreciate it at the time, that was the best parenting advice she ever got.

The other momentous event that happened during those early weeks came about during a night trip to the bathroom. It was John's night to take care of Chelsea. She was having a rough night, so John took her into the bathroom to warm up one of the bottles of milk. Instead of turning on the light, he accidently turned on the fan and instantly, the baby quieted down. She seemed to like the "white noise" that the fan made, so Patty and John decided to install a white noise machine in her room. This small victory helped them to feel that they were finally getting the hang of caring for Chelsea – and just in time, with Patty starting back to work in a few days.

Although six weeks was not enough time, Patty did look forward to having her own life again among her colleagues and away from the baby. Patty would work a condensed work week (four 10-hour days) and "pump" in her office during breaks to make sure John had enough milk for the baby. Then, she would care for Chelsea in the evenings and on weekends so John could have a break, which he often spent hanging out with his poker buddies or preparing for his class.

With Patty constantly hovering every time John cared for the baby, he also looked forward to private time with Chelsea so he could convince Patty, and everyone else, that a father could care for a child just as well as a mother could. Finally, when the semester started again for John, they had John's mother come and care for Chelsea, which was the perfect childcare arrangement. Life finally settled down for the entire family.

The second six months. As the first six months came to an end, John and Patty felt at peace with their ability to care for Chelsea, and a sense of personal accomplishment that they were able to have careers and raise their daughter. Yet, they both felt something was missing in their life. Instead of celebrating their accomplishments, they ended up fighting all the time.

With both Patty and John working all day, there was little time to keep the house as clean as Patty liked or to prepare home-cooked meals. It seemed that Patty's free time was spent working on the house, while John's free time was spent relaxing or playing poker with his friends. Fed up, Patty decided to go on strike and do nothing other than work and care for Chelsea. She said to John, "I QUIT! For now on, if you want something done, you do it." The house was a mess for two weeks until John finally got tired of smelling old shirts in search for a clean one and did a load of laundry. Then, he went shopping and made dinner for the family.

Finally, he approached Patty and said, "OK, you've made your point. The house is a mess and I can't expect you to do everything." The pair proceeded to hash out who would do what and when so that the share of housework was more evenly divided. In the following weeks, Patty also resolved to let go of the control freak in her. In watching John do housework, she realized that there's more than one way to do laundry and to wash dishes. She also found peace in floors that haven't been cleaned in two weeks.

John, on the other hand, began to resent the extra work he was doing. He knew it wasn't fair, but he missed his time relaxing and hanging out with his buddies. More than anything, he missed his wife. While lying down in bed thinking about his life since the birth of the baby, he began wondering about the last time he and Patty had made love. He sat up with a start when he realized it had been eight months since they had sex! Before Chelsea, they would spend Saturday mornings in bed together, talking, laughing, cuddling, and making love. Now, they were lucky to spend five minutes alone together talking about something other than Chelsea. Yet, he looked over at Patty's side of the bed to find it empty, again, because Patty was feeding Chelsea her 4:00 a.m. breakfast. He was determined to change things when Patty returned from the feeding.

Meanwhile, Patty was having similar thoughts. She loved her daughter dearly, but longed for the carefree days when she and John would travel on weekends, go hiking and camping, or just go to dinner and a movie. She also missed their intimate time together, feeling completely disconnected from her marriage. When she returned to the room to talk to her husband, she found him naked, but asleep, on her side of the bed. Instead of waking him, Patty decided to let him sleep, knowing that he had a busy day ahead. She sighed as she put on her robe, quietly slipping downstairs to catch a few precious moments alone with a warm cup of coffee and the front page of the paper.

Case Analysis

As is evident from the case, the Smiths are having a difficult time adjusting to life with Chelsea. Despite having a strong relationship going into the pregnancy, their marriage seemed to falter during that hectic first year. Unlike the other two case studies, where there was more dialogue among family members, the lack of dialogue in this case is not an oversight, but an indication that Patty and John spent most of their time talking about how to take care of Chelsea, rather than each other. Their preparation for Chelsea, in the form of seeking and obtaining information about childbirth, childcare, and breastfeeding, likely helped them troubleshoot the many challenges they faced throughout the pregnancy and early months of Chelsea's life. But although such problem-focused efforts helped them feel in control in advance of Chelsea's arrival, they did little to prepare them for how things actually unfolded or to cope with failed expectations; nor did they help Patty and John know how to identify and face problems that might arise within their relationship. In their attempts to balance childcare duties with their careers, they neglected to care for their marriage.

Patty's need to be in control may have served as an impediment to her own and her husband's transition to parenthood as well, in that she doubted her parenting abilities when things did not work out as she anticipated. She also kept interfering with John's attempts to care for Chelsea, which signaled to John that he was an inadequate caretaker. Such messages, although unintentional, may have furthered the emotional distance between the couple that was already exacerbated by the resentment they felt toward each other. Instead of using communication to help them identify and appraise the difficulties they faced, they avoided addressing the problems in their marriage, resorting to more indirect forms of coping, such as Patty's housework strike, or to aggression (fights).

Ironically, even attempts to address the problem failed, because the couple still focused on other issues, such as John's need to rest, rather than on their marriage. The good news is that both of them recognize there is a problem. Their challenge is to use their troubleshooting abilities to create new routines that allow them to rebuild their relationship.

Questions for Further Analysis

1. Recall the risk and protective factors you read about in the first half of the chapter. What did the Smiths have going for them, and what was working against them?
2. The Smiths faced a number of different challenges throughout their transition to parenthood. Identify the challenges and rank them in order from the most difficult to the least difficult. When making your rankings, consider both the short- and long-term effects on their physical, psychological, and relational health.
3. Review the list again, and rank the stressors in order of how well the Smiths coped with each, from the stressors they handled best to those they handled least well. Make sure you identify the specific coping strategies they used with each stressor (if any) and assess how effectively that particular strategy fulfilled one (or more) of the coping functions (problem-focused, emotion-focused, meaning-focused, relationship-focused, maintenance-focused).
4. Although the Smiths attended classes before their daughter was born, they did not attend any classes afterward. What type of class, if any, do you think the Smiths would benefit from in the post-birth period? If you were to design such a curriculum, what knowledge, skills, and/or abilities would you include?

References

Adler, A. B., Huffman, A. H., Castro, C. A., & Bliese, P. (2005). The impact of deployment length and deployment experience on the wellbeing of male and female military personnel. *Journal of Occupational Health Psychology, 10,* 121–137.

Afifi, T. D., Hutchinson, S., & Krouse, S. (2006). Toward a theoretical model of communal coping in postdivorce families and other naturally occurring groups. *Communication Theory, 16*(3), 378–409.

Afifi, T. D., & Keith, S. (2004). A risk and resiliency model of ambiguous loss in postdivorce stepfamilies. *Journal of Family Communication, 4*(2), 65–98.

Afifi, T. D., & McManus, T. (2010). Communal coping dilemmas in post-divorce families: Introducing meaning back into coping. In R. M. Dailey & B. A. Le Poire (eds), *Applied interpersonal communication matters: Family, health, and community relations* (pp. 67–89). New York: Peter Lang.

Afifi, T. D., McManus, T., Hutchinson, S., & Baker, B. (2007). Parental divorce disclosures, the factors that prompt them, and their impact on parents' and adolescents' well-being. *Communication Monographs, 74,* 78–103.

Afifi, T. D., & Nussbaum, J. F. (2006). Stress and adaptation theories: Families across the life span. In D. O. Braithwaite & L. A. Baxter (eds), *Engaging theories in family communication: Multiple perspectives* (pp. 276–292). Thousand Oaks, CA: Sage.

Afifi, T. D., & Olson, L. (2005). The chilling effect in families and the pressure to conceal secrets. *Communication Monographs, 72,* 192–216.

Afifi, T. D., & Schrodt, P. (2003). "Feeling caught" as a mediator of adolescents' and young adults' avoidance and satisfaction with their parents in divorced and non-divorced households. *Communication Monographs, 70,* 142–173.

Ahlborg, T., & Strandmark, M. (2006). Factors influencing the quality of intimate relationships six months after delivery – First-time parents' own views and coping strategies. *Journal of Psychosomatic Obstetrics & Gynecology, 27,* 163–172.

References

American Cancer Society (2010, September). *What are the key statistics about breast cancer?* Retrieved December 14, 2010 from http://www.cancer.org/Cancer/BreastCancer/DetailedGuide/breast-cancer-key-statistics.

American Pregnancy Association (n.d.). *Statistics.* Retrieved December 5, 2010 from http://www.americanpregnancy.org/main/statistics.html.

American Psychological Association (2009). *Stress in America.* Retrieved March 4, 2011 from http://www.apa.org/news/press/releases/stress-exec-summary.pdf.

American Psychological Association (n.d.). *Mind/body health: Stress.* Retrieved September 10, 2010 from http://www.apa.org/helpcenter/stress.aspx.

Amirkhan, J., & Auyeung, B. (2007). Coping with stress across the lifespan: Absolute vs relative changes in strategy. *Journal of Applied Developmental Psychology, 28,* 298–317.

Angell, R. C. (1936). *The family encounters the Depression.* New York: Scribner.

Appleyard, K., Egeland, B., van Dulmen, M., & Sroufe, L. A. (2005). When more is not better: The role of cumulative risk in child behavior outcomes. *Journal of Child Psychology and Psychiatry, 46,* 235–245.

Aune, K. S., & Comstock, J. (2002). An exploratory investigation of jealousy in the family. *Journal of Family Communication, 2,* 29–39.

Austenfeld, J. L., & Stanton, A. L. (2004). Coping through emotional approach: A new look at emotion, coping, and health-related outcomes. *Journal of Personality, 72,* 1335–1363.

Badr, H., Carmack, C. L., Kashy, D. A., Cristofanilli, M., & Revenson, T. A. (2010). Dyadic coping in metastatic breast cancer. *Health Psychology, 29,* 169–180.

Bailey, S. J. (2003). Challenges and strengths in nonresidential parenting following divorce. *Marriage and Family Review, 35,* 29–44.

Bandura, A. (1986). *Social foundations of thought and action: A social cognitive theory.* Englewood Cliffs, NJ: Prentice-Hall.

Barnes, J., Kroll, L., Lee, J., Jones, A., & Stein, A. (1998). Communication about parental illness with children who have learning disabilities and behavioral problems: Three case studies. *Child: Care, Health, and Development, 24,* 441–456.

Baxter, L. A. (2006). Relational dialectics theory. In D. O. Braithwaite & L. A. Baxter (eds), *Engaging Theories in Family communication* (pp. 130–145).Thousand Oaks, CA: Sage.

Beach, W. A. (2001). Stability and ambiguity: Managing uncertain moments when updating news about mom's cancer. *Text, 21,* 221–250.

Beach, W. A., & Andersen, J. (2003). Communication and cancer? Part I: The noticeable absence of interactional research. *Journal of Psychosocial Oncology, 21,* 1–23.

Berg, C. A., & Upchurch, R. (2007). A developmental-contextual model of couples coping with chronic illness across the adult life span. *Psychological Bulletin, 133,* 920–954.

Bergen, K. M., Kirby, E., & McBride, M. C. (2007). "How do you get two houses cleaned?" Accomplishing family caregiving in commuter marriages. *Journal of Family Communication, 7,* 287–307.

Billings, A. G., & Moos, R. (1981). The role of coping processes and social resources among adults with unipolar depression. *Journal of Behavioral Medicine, 4,* 139–157.

Black, K., & Lobo, M. (2008). A conceptual review of family resilience factors. *Journal of Family Nursing, 13,* 33–55.

Blumer, H. (1969). *Symbolic interactionism: Perspective and method.* Englewood Cliffs, NJ: Prentice Hall.

Bochner, A. P. (2002). Perspectives on inquiry III: The moral of stories. In M. Knapp & J. Daly (eds), *The handbook of interpersonal communication* (3rd edn) (pp. 73–101). Thousand Oaks, CA: Sage.

Bodenmann, G. (1995). A systemic-transactional view of stress and coping in couples. *Swiss Journal of Psychology, 54,* 34–49.

Bodenmann, G. (2005). Dyadic coping and its significance for marital functioning. In T. Revenson, K. Kayser, & G. Bodenmann (eds), *Couples coping with stress: Emerging perspectives on dyadic coping* (pp. 33–50). Washington, DC: American Psychological Association.

Boss, P. (1988). *Family stress management.* Newbury Park, CA: Sage

Boss, P. (1999). *Ambiguous Loss.* Cambridge, MA: Harvard University Press.

Boss, P. (2002). *Family stress management: A contextual approach* (2nd edn). Thousand Oaks, CA: Sage.

Bosticco, C., & Thompson, T. (2005). The role of communication and story telling in the family grieving system. *Journal of Family Communication, 5,* 255–278.

Braithwaite, D. O., & Baxter, L. A. (2006). "You're my parent but you're not": Dialectical tensions in stepchildren's perceptions about communicating with the nonresidential parent. *Journal of Applied Communication Research, 34,* 30–48.

Braithwaite, D. O., & Wood, J. T. (eds). (2000) *Case studies in interpersonal communication: Processes and problems.* Belmont, CA: Wadsworth Publishing.

Brashers, D. E. (2001). Communication and uncertainty management. *Journal of Communication, 51,* 477–497.

Breunlin, D. C. (1988). Oscillation theory and family development. In C. Falicov (ed.), *Family transitions. Continuity and change over the life cycle* (pp. 133–158). New York: The Guilford Press.

Brott, A. A. (2004). *The new father: A dad's guide to the first year* (2nd edn). New York: Abbleville Press.

Brown, R. T., Fuemmeler, B., Anderson, D., Jamieson, S., Simonian, S., Hall, R. K., et al. (2007). Adjustment of children and their mothers with breast cancer. *Journal of Pediatric Psychology, 32,* 297–308.

References

Burgess, E. W. (1926). The family as a unit of interacting personalities. *The Family*, 7, 3–9.

Burleson, B. R., & MacGeorge, E. L. (2002). Supportive communication. In M. Knapp & J. Daly (eds), *Handbook of interpersonal communication* (3rd edn) (pp. 374–422). Thousand Oaks, CA: Sage.

Burr, W. R., Klein, S. R., & colleagues (1994). *Reexamining family stress: New theory and research*. Thousand Oaks, CA: Sage.

Bute, J. J., & Vik, T. A. (2010). Privacy management as unfinished business: Shifting boundaries in the context of infertility. *Communication Studies*, 61, 1–20.

Butler, L. D., Field, N. P., Busch, A. L., Seplaki, J. E., Hastings, T. A., & Spiegel, D. (2005). Anticipating loss and other temporal stressors predict traumatic stress symptoms among partners of metastatic/recurrent breast cancer patients. *Psycho-Oncology*, 14, 492–502.

Butler, J., & Rosenblum, B. (1996). *Cancer in two voices*. Duluth, MN: Spinsters Ink.

Campbell, N. A., & Reece, J. B. (2002). *Biology* (6th edn). New York: Benjamin Cummings.

Canary, D. J., Stafford, L., & Semic, B. A. (2002). A panel study of the associations between maintenance strategies and relational characteristics. *Journal of Marriage and the Family*, 64, 395–406.

Canfield, J., Hansen, M., & Kelly, M. (2006). *Chicken soup for the breast cancer survivor's soul: Stories to inspire, support, and heal*. Deerfield Beach, FL: Health Communications, Inc.

Caplan, S. E., Haslett, B. J., & Burleson, B. R. (2005). Telling it like it is: The adaptive function of narratives in coping with loss in later life. *Health Communication*, 17, 233–251.

Carter, B. (1999). Becoming parents: The family with young children. In B. Barter & M. McGoldrick (eds), *The expanded family life cycle: Individual, family, and social perspectives* (pp. 249–273). Boston, MA: Allyn and Bacon.

Carter, B., & McGoldrick, M. (1999). The expanded family life cycle: Individual, family, and social perspectives. In B. Barter & M. McGoldrick (eds), *The expanded family life cycle: Individual, family, and social perspectives* (pp. 1–26). Boston, MA: Allyn and Bacon.

Castle, H., Slade, P., Barranco-Wadlow, M., & Rogers, M. (2008). Attitudes to emotional expression, social support, and postnatal adjustment in new parents. *Journal of Reproductive and Infant Psychology*, 26, 180–194.

Caughlin, J.P., & Afifi, T. D. (2004). When is topic avoidance unsatisfying? Examining moderators of the association between avoidance and dissatisfaction. *Human Communication Research*, 30, 479–513.

Caughlin, J. P., & Huston, T. L. (2002). A contextual analysis of the association between demand/withdraw and marital satisfaction. *Personal Relationships*, 9, 95–119.

References

Cavan, R. S., & Ranck, K. H. (1938). *The family and the Depression: A study of one hundred Chicago families.* Chicago: University of Chicago Press.

Center for Disease Control (2007). *Deaths: Final data for 2007.* National Vital Statistics Reports, 58(19). Retrieved March 16, 2011 from http://www.cdc.gov/NCHS/data/nvsr/nvsr58/nvsr58_19.pdf.

Cohen, F., & Lazarus, R. S. (1973). Active coping processes, coping dispositions, and recovery from surgery. *Psychosomatic Medicine, 35,* 375–389.

Colaner, C., & Kranstuber, H. (2010). 'Forever kind of wondering': Communicatively managing uncertainty in adoptive families. *Journal of Family Communication, 10,* 236–255.

Compas, B. E., Connor-Smith, J. K., Saltzman, H., Thomsen, A. H., & Wadsworth, M. E. (2001). Coping with stress during childhood and adolescence: Problems, progress, and potential in theory and research. *Psychological Bulletin, 127,* 87–127.

Compas, B. E., Worsham, N. L., Epping-Jordan, J. E., Grant, K. E., Mireault, G., Howell, D. C., et al. (1994). *Health Psychology, 13,* 507–515.

Copeland, D. B., & Harbaugh, B. L. (2010). Psychological differences related to parenting infants among single and married mothers. *Issues in Comprehensive Pediatric Nursing, 33,* 129–148.

Coyne, J. C., Ellard, J. H., & Smith, D. A. F. (1990). Social support, interdependence, and the dilemmas of helping. In B. Sarason, I. Sarason, & Pierce, G. (eds), *Social support: An interactional view* (pp. 129–149). New York: John Wiley.

Coyne, J. C., & Fiske, V. (1992). Couples coping with chronic and catastrophic illness. In T. J. Akamatsu, M. A. P. Stephens, S. E. Hobfoll, & J. H. Crowther (eds), *Family health psychology* (pp. 129–150). Washington, DC: Hemisphere.

Coyne, J. C., & Smith, D. A. F. (1991). Couples coping with a myocardial infarction: A contextual perspective on wives' distress. *Journal of Personality and Social Psychology, 61,* 404–412.

Cunningham, M. R., Shamblen, S. R., Barbee, A P., & Ault, L. K. (2005). Social allergies in romantic relationships: Behavioral repetition, emotional sensitization, and dissatisfaction in dating couples. *Personal Relationships, 12,* 273–295.

Curan, M., Hazen, N., Jacobvitz, D., & Feldman, A. (2005). Representations of early family relationships predict marital maintenance during the transition to parenthood. *Journal of Family Psychology, 19,* 189–197.

Dailey, R. M., Lee, C. M., & Spitzberg, B. H. (2007). Communicative aggression: Toward a more interactional view of psychological abuse. In B. H. Spitzberg & W. R. Cupach (eds), *The dark side of interpersonal communication* (2nd edn) (pp. 297–326). Mahwah, NJ: Erlbaum.

Davey, M., Gulish, L., Askew, J., Godette, K., & Childs, N. (2005). Adolescents coping with mom's breast cancer: Developing family intervention programs. *Journal of Marital and Family Therapy, 31,* 247–258.

References

Dawalt, S. (2007). *365 deployment days: A wife's survival story*. Austin, TX: Bridgeway Books.

DeLongis, A., & O'Brien, T. (1990). An interpersonal framework for stress and coping: An application to the families of Alzheimer's patients. In M. Stephens, J. Crowther, S. Hobfoll, & Tennenbaum (eds), *Stress and coping in later-life families* (pp. 221–240). New York: Hemisphere Press.

Dennis, M. R., Kunkel, A., & Keyton, J. (2008). Problematic integration theory, appraisal theory, and the Bosom Buddy Cancer Support Group. *Journal of Applied Communication Research, 36*, 415–436.

Dickson, F. C., Christian, A., & Remmo, C. J. (2004). An exploration of marital and family issues among later-life adults. In A. Vangelisti (ed.), *Handbook of family communication* (pp. 153–174). Mahwah, NJ: Erlbaum.

Dimiceli, E. E., Steinhardt, M. A., & Smith, S. E. (2010). Stressful experiences, coping strategies, and predictors of health-related outcomes among wives of deployed military servicemen. *Armed Forces & Society, 36*, 351–373.

Di Nola, G. M. (2008). Factors afflicting families during military deployment. *Military Medicine, 172*, v–vii.

Dolan, C. A., & Ender, M. G. (2008). The coping paradox: Work, stress, and coping in the US Army. *Military Psychology, 20*, 151–169.

Donovan-Kicken, E., & Caughlin, J. P. (2010). A multiple goals perspective on topic avoidance and relationship satisfaction in the context of breast cancer. *Communication Monographs, 77*, 231–256.

Doss, B. D., Rhoades, G. K., Stanley, S. M., & Markman, H. J. (2009). The effect of the transition to parenthood on relationship quality: An 8-year prospective study. *Journal of Personality and Social Psychology, 96*, 601–619.

Drummet, A. R., Coleman, M., & Cable, S. (2003). Military families under stress: Implications for family life education. *Family Relations, 52*, 279–287.

Dunivin, K. O. (1994). Military culture: Change and continuity. *Armed Forces and Society, 20*, 531–547.

Dun, T. (2010). Turning points in parent-grandparent relationships during the start of a new generation. *Journal of Family Communication, 10*, 194–210.

Dupuis, S. B. (2009). An ecological examination of older remarried couples. *Journal of Divorce & Remarriage, 50*(6), 369–387.

Dysart-Gale, D. (2007). Respite: Cultural values in North American and Caribbean caregiving. *Canadian Journal of Communication, 32*, 401–415.

Edwards, J. R., & Cooper, C. L. (1988). The impacts of positive psychological states on physical health: A review and theoretical framework. *Social Science Medicine, 27*, 1447–1459.

Faber, A. J., Willerton, E., Clymer, S. R., MacDermid, S. M., & Weiss, H. M. (2008). Ambiguous absence, ambiguous presence: A qualitative study of military reserve families in wartime. *Journal of Family Psychology, 22*, 222–230.

Family (1989). *Cambridge Dictionary Online*. Cambridge University Press.

References

Retrieved September 10, 2010 from http://dictionary.cambridge.org/dictionary/british/family_1.

Family. (n.d.). *Meriam-Webster*. Encyclopedia Britannica Company. Retrieved September 10, 2010 from http://www.merriam-webster.com/dictionary/family.

Family. (n.d.). In D. Harper (ed.), *Online etymology dictionary*. Retrieved September 10, 2010 from http://www.etymonline.com/index.php?term=family.

Family. (1989). *Oxford English Dictionary* (2nd edn). Oxford University Press. Retrieved September 10, 2010 from http://www.oed.com:80/Entry/67975.

Fiese, B. H., & Pratt, M. W. (2004). Metaphors and meanings of family stories: Integrating life course and systems perspectives on narratives. In M. Pratt & B. Fiese (eds), *Family stories and the lifecourse: Across time and generation* (pp. 401–418). Mahway, NJ: Lawrence Erlbaum.

Fisher, C. L. (2010). Coping with breast cancer across adulthood: Emotional support communication in the mother-daughter bond. *Journal of Applied Communication Research, 38*, 386–411.

Fisher, W. R. (1987). *Human communication as a narration: Toward a philosophy of reason, value, and action*. Columbia, SC: University of South Carolina Press.

Fitzpatrick, M. A., & Caughlin, J. P. (2002). Interpersonal communication in family relationships. In M. L. Knapp & J. A. Daly (eds), *Handbook of interpersonal communication* (3rd edn) (pp. 726–778). Thousand Oaks, CA: Sage.

Fitzpatrick, M. A., & Ritchie, L. D. (1994). Communication schemata within the family: Multiple perspectives on family interaction. *Human Communication Research, 20*, 275–301.

Flake, E. M., Davis, B. E., Johnson, P. L., & Middleton, L. S. (2009). The psycho-social effects of deployment on military children. *Journal of Developmental & Behavioral Pediatrics, 30*, 271–278.

Floyd, K. (2006). Human affection exchange: XII. Affectionate communication is associated with diurnal variation in salivary free cortisol. *Western Journal of Communication, 70*, 47–63.

Floyd, K., & Afifi, T. D. (2011). *Biological and physiological perspectives on interpersonal communication*. In M. Knapp & J. Daly (eds), *The handbook of interpersonal communication* (4th edn, pp. 87–128). Thousand Oaks, CA: Sage.

Floyd, K., Mikkelson, A. C., Tafoya, M. A., Farinelli, L., La Valley, A. G., Judd, J., Haynes, M. T., Davis, K. L., & Wilson, J. (2007). Human affection exchange: XIII. Affectionate communication accelerates neuroendocrine stress recovery. *Health Communication, 22*, 123–132.

Floyd, K., & Pauley, P. M. (2011). Affectionate communication is good, except when it isn't: On the dark side of expressing affection. In W. Cupach & B. Spitzberg (eds), *The dark side of close relationships II* (pp. 145–174). New York: Routledge.

Folkman, S. (2008). The case for positive emotions in the stress process. *Anxiety, Stress, & Coping, 21*(1), 3–14.

References

Folkman, S., & Lazarus, R. S. (1985). If it changes it must be a process: Study of emotion and coping during three stages of a college examination. *Journal of Personality and Social Psychology, 48*, 150–170.

Folkman, S., & Lazarus, R. (1991). Coping and emotion. In A. Monat & R. Lazarus (eds), *Stress and coping: An anthology* (pp. 207–227). New York: Columbia University Press.

Folkman, S., Lazarus, R. S., Dunkel-Schetter, C., DeLongis, A., & Gruen, R. J. (1986). Dynamics of a stressful encounter: Cognitive appraisal, coping, and encounter outcomes. *Journal of Personality and Social Psychology, 50*, 992–1003.

Folkman, S., & Moskowitz, J. T. (2004). Coping: Pitfalls and promise. *Annual Review of Psychology, 55*, 745–774.

Fredrickson, B. L. (2001). The role of positive emotions in positive psychology: The broaden-and-build theory of positive emotions. *American Psychologist, 56*, 218–226.

Galvin, K., Dickson, F. C., & Marrow, S. F. (2006). Systems theory: Patterns and (w)holes in family communication. In D. O. Braithwaite & L. A. Baxter, (eds), *Engaging theories in family communication: Multiple perspectives* (pp. 309–324). Thousand Oaks, CA: Sage.

Galvin, K. M., Bylund, C. L., & Brommel, B. J. (2008). *Family communication: Cohesion and change* (7th edn). Boston: Pearson.

Gameiro, S., Boivin, J., Canavarro, M. C., Mauda-Ramos, M., & Soares, I. (2010). *Journal of Family Psychology, 24*, 175–187.

Gardner, K. A., & Cutrona, C. E. (2004). Social support communication in families. In A. L. Vangelisti (ed.), *Handbook of family communication* (pp. 495–512). Mahwah, NJ: Erlbaum.

Gergen, K., & Davis, K. E. (1985). *The social construction of the person.* New York: Springer-Verlag.

Golden, A. G. (2001). Modernity and the communicative management of multiple roles: The case of the worker-parent. *Journal of Family Communication, 1*, 233–264.

Goldsmith, D. J. (2004). *Communicating social support.* New York: Cambridge University Press.

Graham, J. M., & Conoley, C. L. (2006). The role of marital atttibutions in the relationship between life stressors and marital quality. *Personal Relationships, 13*, 231–241.

Grzywacz, J. G., & Almeida, D. M. (2008). Stress and binge drinking: A daily process examination of stressor pile-up and socioeconomic status is affect regulation. *International Journal of Stress Management, 15*, 364–380.

Guidotti, T. L. (2000). Firefighters, stress in. In G. Fink (ed.), *Encyclopedia of stress* (pp. 146–149). San Diego, CA: Academic Press.

Gump, B. B., & Matthews, K.A. (1999). Do background stressors influence

References

reactivity to and recovery from acute stressors? *Journal of Applied Social Psychology, 29*, 469–494.

Hampel, P., & Petermann, F. (2005). Age and gender effects on coping in children and adolescents. *Journal of Youth and Adolescence, 34*, 73–83.

Harburg, E., Kaciroti, N., Gleiberman, L., Julius, M., & Schork, M. A. (2008). Marital pair anger-coping types may act as an entity to affect mortality: Preliminary findings from a prospective study (Tecumseh, Michigan, 1971–1988). *Journal of Family Communication, 8*, 44–61.

Harris, J., Bowen, D. J., Badr, H., Hannon, P., Hay, J., & Sterba, R. (2009). Family communication during the cancer experience. *Journal of Health Communication, 14*, 76–84.

Harzold, E., & Sparks, L. (2006). Adult child perceptions of communication and humor when the parent is diagnosed with cancer: A suggestive perspective from communication theory. *Qualitative Research Reports in Communication, 7*(1), 67–78.

Hay, C., Meldrum, R., & Mann, K. (2010). Traditional bullying, cyber bullying, and deviance: A general strain theory approach. *Journal of Contemporary Criminal Justice, 26*, 130–147.

Henderson, K. (2006). *While they're at war: The true story of the American family in the homefront.* New York: Houghton Mifflin.

Hill, R. (1949). *Families under stress: Adjustment to the crises of war separation and reunion.* New York: Harper & Brothers.

Hill, R. (1958). Generic features of families under stress. *Social Casework, 39*, 139–150.

Hill, R., & Hansen, D. A. (1960). The identification of conceptual frameworks utilized in family study. *Marriage and Family Living, 22*, 299–311.

Hilton, E. A., Crawford, J. A., & Tarko, M. A. (2000). Men's perspectives on individual and family coping with their wives' breast cancer and chemotherapy. *Western Journal of Nursing Research, 22*, 438–459.

Hilton, B. A., & Koop, P. M. (1994). Family communication patterns in coping with early breast cancer. *Western Journal of Nursing Research, 16*, 366–391.

Hobfoll, S. E., et al. (1991). War-related stress: Addressing the stress of war and other traumatic events. *American Psychologist, 46*(8), 848–855.

Hobfoll, S. E., Dunahoo, C. L., Ben-Porath, Y., & Monnier, J. (1994). Gender and coping: The dual-axis model of coping. *American Journal of Community Psychology, 22*, 49–81.

Hofstede, G. (2001). *Culture's consequences: Comparing values, behaviors, institutions, and organizations across nations.* Thousand Oaks, CA: Sage.

Holahan, C. J., & Moos, R. H. (1987). Personal and contextual determinants of coping strategies. *Journal of Personality and Social Psychology, 52*, 946–955.

Holmes, T. H., & Rahe, R. H. (1967). The social readjustment scale. *Journal of Psychosomatic Research, 11*, 213–218.

Huang, M. P., & Alessi, N. E. (1999). Presence as an emotional experience. In

References

J. D. Westwood, H. M. Hoffman, R. A. Robb, and D. Stredney (eds), *Medicine meets virtual reality: The convergence of physical and informational technologies options for a new era in health care* (148–15). Amsterdam: IOS Press.

Hughes, C., Lerman, C., Schwartz, M., Peshkin, B. N., Wenzel, L., Narod, S., et al. (2001). All in the family: Evaluation of the process and content of sisters' communication about BRCA1 and BRCA2 genetic test results. *American Journal of Medical Genetics, 107*, 143–150.

Hummelinck, A., & Pollock, K. (2006). Parents' information needs about the treatment of their chronically ill child: A qualitative study. *Patient Education and Counseling, 62*(2), 228–234.

Huston, T. L., & Holmes, E. K. (2004). Becoming parents. *Handbook of family communication* (pp. 105–134). Mahwah, NJ: Lawrence Erlbaum Associates.

Huston, T. L., & Vangelisti, A. L. (1995). How parenthood affects marriage. In M. A. Fitzpatrick & A. L. Vangelisti (eds), *Explaining family interactions* (pp. 147–176). Thousand Oaks, CA: Sage.

Infante, D. A., Chandler, T. A., & Rudd, J. E. (1989). Test of an argumentative skill deficiency model of interspousal violence. *Communication Monographs, 56*, 163–177.

Iovine, V. (1997). *The girlfriend's guide to surviving the first year of motherhood.* New York: Penguin Putnam.

Johnson, M. P. (1995). Patriarchal terrorism and common couple violence: Two forms of violence against women. *Journal of Marriage and the Family, 57*, 283–294.

Jones, D. J., Beach, S. R. H., & Jackson, H. (2004). Family influences on health: A framework to organize research and guide intervention. *Handbook of family communication* (pp. 647–672). Mahwah, NJ: Lawrence Erlbaum Associates.

Joseph, A. L., & Afifi, T. D. (2010). Military wives' stressful disclosures to their deployed husbands: The role of protective buffering. *Journal of Applied Communication Research, 38*, 412–434.

Karney, B. R., & Crown, J. S. (2007). *Families under stress: An assessment of data, theory, and research on marriage and divorce in the military.* (MG-599-OSD). Santa Monica, CA: RAND Corporation.

Karney, B., Story, L., & Bradbury, T. (2005). Marriages in context: Interactions between chronic and acute stress among newlyweds. In T. Revenson, K. Kayser & G. Bodenmann (eds), *Couples coping with stress: Emerging perspectives on couples coping with stress* (pp. 13–32). Washington, DC: American Psychological Association.

Kayser, K., Watson, L. E., & Andrade, J. T. (2007). Cancer as a "we-disease": Examining the process of coping from a relational perspective. *Family, Systems, & Health, 25*, 404–418.

Keefe, M. R., Karlsen, K. K., Lobo, M. L., Kotzer, A. M., & Dudley, W. D. (2006). Reducing parenting stress in families with irritable infants. *Nursing Research, 55*, 198–205.

References

Keitner, G., Heru, A., & Glick, I. (2010) *Clinical manual of couples and family therapy*. Washington DC: Guilford Press.

Keizer, R., Dykstra, P. A., & Poortman, A.-R. (2010). The transition to parenthood and well-being: The impact of partner status and work hour transitions. *Journal of Family Psychology, 24*, 429–438.

Kluwer, E. S., & Johnson, M. D. (2007). Conflict frequency and relationship quality across the transition to parenthood. *Journal of Marriage and Family, 69*, 1089–1106.

Knapp, M. L. (2008). *Lying and deception in human interaction*. Boston: Pearson Education: Allyn & Bacon.

Knobloch, L. K. (2008). The content of relational uncertainty within marriage. *Journal of Social and Personal Relationships, 25*, 467–495.

Knox, J., & Price, D. H. (1999). Total force and the new American military family: Implications for social work practice. *Families in Society: Journal of Contemporary Human Services, 80*, 128–136.

Koenig Kellas, J. (2005). Family ties: Communicating identity through jointly told stories. *Communication Monographs, 72*, 365–389.

Koenig Kellas, J., & Trees, A. R. (2006). Finding meaning in difficult family experiences: Interaction processes during joint family storytelling. *Journal of Family Communication, 6*, 49–76.

Koenig Kellas, J., Trees, A. R., Schrodt, P., LeClair-Underberg, C., & Willer, E. K. (2010). Exploring links between well-being and interactional sense-making in married couples' jointly told stories of stress. *Journal of Family Communication, 10*, 174–193.

Koerner, A. F., & Fitzpatrick, M. A. (1997). Family type and conflict: The impact of conversation orientation and conformity orientation on conflict in the family. *Communication Studies, 48*, 59–75.

Kowalski, R. M. (2007). Teasing and bullying. In B. H. Spitzberg & W. R. Cupach (eds). *The dark side of interpersonal communication* (2nd edn, pp. 169–197). Hillsdale, NJ: Lawrence Erlbaum.

Krouse, S. S., & Afifi, T. D. (2007). Family-to-work spillover stress: Coping communicatively in the workplace. *Journal of Family Communication, 7*, 85–122.

Langellier, K. M., & Peterson, E. E. (2004). *Storytelling in daily life: Performing narrative*. Philadelphia, PA: Temple University.

Langer, A., Lawrence, E., & Barry, R. A. (2008). Using a vulnerability-stress-adaptation framework to predict physical aggression trajectories in newlywed marriage. *Journal of Consulting and Clinical Psychology, 76*, 756–768.

Laursen, B., & Collins, W. A. (2004). Parent–child communication during adolescence. In A. Vangelisti (ed.), *Handbook of family communication* (pp. 333–349). Mahwah, NJ: Lawrence Erlbaum.

Lazarus, R. S. (1966). *Psychological stress and the coping process*. New York: McGraw Hill.

References

Lazarus, R. S. (1993). Coping theory and research: Past, present, and future. *Psychosomatic Medicine, 55*, 234–247.

Lazarus, R. S. (1999). *Stress and emotion: A new synthesis.* New York: Springer.

Lazarus, R. S., & Folkman, S. (1984). *Stress, appraisal, and coping.* New York: McGraw-Hill.

Lebel, S., Rosberger, Z., Edgar, L., & Devins, G. M. (2007). *Journal of Psychosomatic Research, 63*, 225–232.

Lee, M. (2009). A path analysis on elder abuse by family caregivers: Applying the ABCX Model. *Journal of Family Violence, 24*, 1–9.

Leiter, M.P., & Durup, J. (1996). Work, home, and in-between: A longitudinal study of spillover. *Journal of Applied Behavioral Science, 32*, 29–47.

LeMasters, E. E. (1957). Parenthood as crisis. *Marriage and Family Living, 19*, 352–355.

Levy-Shiff, R., Dimitrovsky, L., Shulman, S., & Har-Even, D. (1998). Cognitive appraisals, coping strategies, and support resources as correlates of parenting and infant development. *Developmental Psychology, 34*, 1417–1427.

Levy-Shiff, R., Goldshmidt, I., & Har-Even, D. (1991). Transition to parenthood in adoptive families. *Developmental Psychology, 27*, 131–140.

Lewis, T. J., & Manusov, V. (2009). Listening to another's distress in everyday relationships. *Communication Quarterly, 57*, 282–301.

Link, J. (2000). *Breast cancer survival manual (4th edn): A step-by-step guide for the woman with newly diagnosed breast cancer.* New York: Henry Holt.

Lohr, J. M., Olatunji, B. O., Baumeister, R. F., & Bushman, B. J. (2007). The psychology of anger venting and empirically supported alternatives that do no harm. *The Scientific Review of Health Practices, 5*(1), 53–64.

Loutzenhiser, L., & Sevigny, P. R. (2008). Infant sleep and the quality of family life for the first-time parents of three-month-old infants. *Fathering, 6*, 2–19.

Lyons, R. F., Mickelson, K. D., Sullivan, M. J. L., & Coyne, J. C. (1998). Coping as a communal process. *Journal of Social and Personal Relationships, 15*, 579–605.

McCubbin, H. I. (1979). Integrating coping behavior in family stress theory. *Journal of Marriage and the Family, 41*, 237–244.

McCubbin, H. I., Boss, P., Wilson, L.R., & Lester, G. (1980). Developing family invulnerability to stress: Coping patterns and strategies wives employ in managing family separations. In J. Trost (ed.), *The family in change* (pp. 186–173). Vasteras, Sweden: International Library.

McCubbin, H. I., Dahl, B. B., & Hunter, E. J. (1976). Research on the military family: A review. In H. McCubbin, B. Dahl, & E. Hunter (eds), *Families in the military system* (pp. 291–319). Beverly Hills, CA: Sage.

McCubbin, H. I., Joy, C., Cauble, A., Comeau, J., Patterson, J., & Needle, R. (1980). Family stress and coping: A decade review. *Journal of Marriage and the Family, 42*, 855–871.

McCubbin, H. I., Larsen, A. S., & Olsen, D. H. (1982). Family coping strategies.

References

In H. McCubbin, A. Laresen, and D. Olsen (eds), *Family inventories* (pp. 101–120). St. Paul, Minnesota: University of Minnesota.

McCubbin, H. I., & Patterson, J. M. (1983). The family stress process: The Double ABCX Model of Adjustment and Adaptation. *Marriage & Family Review, 6,* 7–37.

McFarlane, A. C. (2009). Military deployment: The impact on children and family adjustment and the need for care. *Current Opinion in Psychiatry, 22,* 369–373.

McKay, K., Ross, L. E., & Goldberg, A. E. (2010). Adaptation to parenthood during the post-adoption period: A review of the literature. *Adoption Quarterly, 13,* 125–144.

McKenna, M. C., Zevon, M. A., Corn, B., & Rounds, J. (1999). Psychosocial factors and the development of breast cancer: A meta-analysis. *Health Psychology, 18,* 520–531.

McLaren, R. M., & Solomon, D. H. (2008). Appraisal and distancing responses in response to hurtful messages. *Communication Research, 35,* 339–357.

McNulty, P. A. (2005). Reported stressors and health care needs of active duty Navy personnel during three phases of deployment in support of the war in Iraq. *Military Medicine, 170,* 530–535.

Maguire, K. (2007). Will it ever end? A (re)examination of uncertainty in college student premarital long-distance romantic relationships. *Communication Quarterly, 55,* 415–432.

Maguire, K., & Kinney, T. (2010). When distance is problematic: Communication and coping in women's stressful long distance dating relationships. *Journal of Applied Communication Research, 38,* 27–46.

Maguire, K., & Sahlstein, E. (2009). Pro-social, a-social, and anti-social coping in long distance romantic relationships. In T. Kinney & M. Porhola (eds), *Current advances in anti- & pro-social communication: An examination of theories, methods, and applications* (pp. 127–138). New York: Peter Lang.

Maguire, K., & Sahlstein, E. (in press). In the line of fire: Family management of acute stress during wartime deployment. In F. Dickson & L. Webb (eds), *Families in crisis: Effective communication for managing unexpected, negative events.* Cresskill, NJ: Hampton Press.

Maguire, K., & Sahlstein, E. (2001). *Under the gun: Army wives' use of individual, social, and communal coping in the context of a wartime deployment.* Paper presented at the annual meeting of the International Communication Association, May 2011 (Boston).

Malis, R. S., & Roloff, M. E. (2006). Features of serial arguing and coping strategies: Links with stress and well-being. In R. M. Dailey & B. A. Le Poire (eds) *Applied interpersonal communication matters: Family, health, and community relations.* (pp. 39–65). New York, NY: Peter Lang.

Mallinger, J. B., Griggs, J. J., & Shields, C. G. (2006). Family communication and mental health after breast cancer. *European Journal of Cancer Care, 15*, 355–361.

Manne, S., Ostroff, J., Rini, C., Fox, K., Goldstein, L., & Grana, G. (2004). The interpersonal process model of intimacy: The role of self-disclosure, partner disclosure, and partner responsiveness in interactions between breast cancer patients and their partners. *Journal of Family Psychology, 18*, 589–599.

Menaghan, E. G. (1983). Individual coping efforts and family studies: Conceptual and methodological issues. *Marriage and Family Review, 6*, 113–135.

Menninger, K. A. (1963). *The vital balance: The life processes of mental health and illness.* New York: Viking Press.

Mental Health America (2006). *Americans reveal top stressors, how they cope.* Retrieved October 20, 2010 from http://www.mentalhealthamerica.net/index.cfm?objectid=ABD3DC4E-1372–4D20-C8274399C9476E26.

Mercer, R. T., & Ferketich, S. L. (1990). Predictors of family functioning eight months following birth. *Nursing Research, 39*, 76–82.

Merolla, A. J. (2010). Relational maintenance during military deployment: Perspectives of wives of deployed US soldiers. *Journal of Applied Communication Research, 38*, 4–26.

Metts, S. (1994). Relational transgressions. In W. Cupach & B. Spitzberg (eds), *The darkside of interpersonal communication* (pp. 217–240). Hillsdale, NJ: Lawrence Erlbaum.

Miller, M. A., & Rahe, R. H. (1997). Life changes scaling for the 1990s. *Journal of Psychosomatic Research, 43*, 279–292.

Miller, B. C., & Sollie, D. L. (1980). Normal stresses during the transition to parenthood. *Family Relations, 29*, 459–465.

Mitnick, D. M., Heyman, R. E., & Smith Slep, A. M. (2009). Changes in relationship satisfaction across the transition to parenthood: A meta-analysis. *Journal of Family Psychology, 23*, 848–852.

Moelker, R., & van der Kloet, I. (2006). Military families and the armed forces. In G. Caforio (ed.), *Handbook of sociology of the military* (pp. 201–223). New York: Springer.

Montalvo, F. F. (1976). Family separation in the Army: A study of the problems encountered and the caretaking resources used by career Army families undergoing military separation. In H. McCubbin, B. Dahl, & E. Hunter (eds), *Families in the military system* (pp. 147–173). Beverly Hills, CA: Sage.

Murkoff, H., & Mazel, S. (2008). *What to expect when you're expecting* (4th edn). New York: Workman.

Murkoff, H., Eisenberg, A., Mazel, S., & Hathaway, S. (2009). *What to expect the first year.* New York: Workman.

Nezu, C. M., Nezu, A. M., Friedman, S. H., Houts, P. S., Dellicarpini, L. A., & Faddis, S. (1999). Cancer and psychological distress. *Journal of Psychosocial Oncology, 16*(3), 27–40.

References

National Conference of State Legislatures (2010). *State unemployment rates: 2010*. Retrieved July 13, 2011, from http://www.ncsl.org/?tabid=20192.

National Military Family Association (2004). *Serving the home front: An analysis of military family support*. Retrieved January 26, 2011, from www.alaskapta.org/NMFAServingthehomefrontreport.pdf.

National Military Family Association (2005). *Report on the cycles of deployment: An analysis of survey responses from April through September 2005*. Retrieved July 27th, 2010, from http://www.nmfa.org/site/DocServer/NMFACyclesofDeployment9.pdf?docID=5401.

Nixon, P. G. F. (1976). The human function curve: With special reference to cardiovascular disorders, part I. *The Practitioner, 217*, 765–770.

Noller, P. (1995). Parent-adolescent relationships. In M. Fitzpatrick & A. Vangelisti (eds), *Explaining family interaction* (pp. 77–111). London: Sage.

Norwood, A. E., Fullerton, C. S., & Hagen, K. P. (1996). Those left behind: Military families. In R. J. Ursano & A. E. Norwood (eds), *Emotional aftermath of the Persian Gulf War: Veterans, families, communities, and nations* (pp. 163–197). Washington, DC: American Psychiatric Press, Inc.

Numeroff, L., Harpham, W., & McPhail, D. (2001). *The hope tree: Kids talk about breast cancer*. New York: Simon & Schuster Children's Publishing.

O'Brien, M. L., Buikstra, E., Fallon, T., & Hegney, D. (2009) Strategies for success: A toolbox of coping strategies used by breastfeeding women. *Journal of Clinical Nursing. 18*(11), 1574–1582.

Obrist, P. A. (1981). *Cardiovascular psychophysiology: A perspective*. New York: Plenum.

Odom, S. L., & Chandler, L. (1990). Transition to parenthood for parents and technology-assisted infants. *Topics in Early Childhood Special Education, 9*, 43–54.

Olson, L. N. (2002). Exploring "common couple violence" in heterosexual romantic relationships. *Western Journal of Communication, 66*, 104–129.

Olson, L. N. (2004). The role of voice in the (re)construction of a battered woman's identity: An autoethnography of one woman's experiences of abuse. *Women's Studies in Communication, 27*, 1–33.

Orthner, D. K., & Rose, R. (2003). Dealing with the effects of absence: Deployment and adjustment to separation among military families. *Journal of Family and Consumer Science, 95*, 33–37.

Palmer, C. (2008). A theory of risk and resilience factors in military families. *Military Psychology, 20*, 205–217.

Park, C. L. (2010). Making meaning of the meaning literature: An integrative review of meaning making and its effects on adjustment to stressful life events. *Psychological Bulletin, 136*, 257–301.

Patterson, J. M. (1988). Families experiencing stress. *Family Systems Medicine, 6*, 202–237.

References

Patterson, J. M. (2002). Integrating family resilience and family stress theory. *Journal of Marriage and the Family, 64*, 349–360.

Patterson, J. M., & Garwick, A. W. (1994). Levels of meaning in family stress theory. *Family Process, 33*, 287–304.

Patterson, J. M., & McCubbin, H. I. (1984). Gender roles and coping. *Journal of Marriage and the Family, 46*, 95–104.

Paul, E. L., Poole, A., & Jakubowyc, N. (1998). Intimacy development and romantic status: Implications for adjustment to the college transition. *Journal of College Student Development, 39*, 75–86.

Pavlicin, K. M. (2007). *Life after deployment: Military families share reunion stories and advice.* St. Paul, Minnesota: Elva Resa.

Pearce, W. B., & Cronen, V. E. (1980). *Communication, action, and meaning: The creation of social realities.* New York: Praeger.

Pearlin, L. I. (1983). Role strains and personal stress. In H. Kaplan (ed.), *Psychosocial stress in theory and research* (pp. 3–32). New York: Academic Press.

Pearlin, L. I., & Schooler, C. (1978). The structure of coping. *Journal of Health and Social Behavior, 19*, 2–21.

Penly, J. A., Tomaka, J., & Wieb, J. S. (2002). The association of coping to physical and psychological health outcomes: A meta-analytic review. *Journal of Behavioral Medicine, 25*, 551–603.

Philipsen, G. (1992). *Speaking culturally: Explorations in social communication.* Albany, NY: State University of New York Press.

Pinquart, M., & Teubert, D. (2010). Effects of parenting education with expectant and new parents: A meta-analysis. *Journal of Family Psychology, 24*, 316–327.

Pistrang, N., & Barker, C. (2005). How partners talk in times of stress: A process analysis approach. In T. A. Revenson, K. Kayser, & G. Bodenmann (eds), *Couples coping with stress: Emerging perspectives on dyadic coping* (pp. 97–119). Washington, DC: American Psychological Association.

Powell, K. A., & Afifi, T. D. (2005). Uncertainty management and adoptees' ambiguous loss of their birth parents. *Journal of Social and Personal Relationships, 22*, 129–151.

Priem, J., McLaren, R. M., & Solomon, D. H. (2010). Relational messages, perceptions of hurt, and biological stress reactions to a disconfirming interaction. *Communication Research, 37*, 48–72.

Purdy, I. B. (2010). Social, cultural, and medical factors that influence maternal breastfeeding. *Issues in Mental Health Nursing, 31*, 365–367.

Radina, M. E., & Armer, J. M. (2001). Post-breast cancer lymphedema and the family: A qualitative investigation of families coping with chronic illness. *Journal of Family Nursing, 7*, 281–299.

Rahe, R. H. (1975). Epidemiological studies of life change and illness. In J. Lipowski, D. Lipsitt, & P. Whybrow (eds), *Psychosomatic medicine: Current trends and clinical applications* (pp. 421–434). New York: Oxford University Press.

Ray, S. L., & Vanstone, M. (2009). The impact of PTSD on veterans' family relationships: An interpretive phenomenological inquiry. *International Journal of Nursing Studies, 46*, 838–847.

Reiter, M. J., & Gee, C. B. (2008). Open communication and partner support in intercultural and interfaith romantic relationships: A relational maintenance approach. *Journal of Social and Personal Relationships, 25*, 539–559.

Repetti, R. L., & Wood, J. (1997). Families accommodating to chronic stress: Unintended and unnoticed processes. In B. H. Gottlieb (ed.), *Coping with chronic stress* (pp. 191–220). New York: Plenum Publishing Corp.

Revenson, T. A., Kayser, K., & Bodenmann, G. (2005). Introduction. In T. Revenson, K. Kayser, and G. Bodenmann (eds), *Couples coping with stress: Emerging perspectives on dyadic coping* (pp. 3–10). Washington, DC: American Psychological Association.

Reznik, R. M., Roloff, M. E., & Miller, C. (2010). Communication during interpersonal arguing: Implications for stress symptoms. *Argumentation & Advocacy, 46*, 193–213.

Richardson, G. E. (2002). The metatheory of resilience and resiliency. *Journal of Clinical Psychology, 58*, 307–321.

Ritchie, L. D. (1991). What the instrument says: An elaborated theory of family communication patterns. *Communication Research, 18*, 175–187.

Roesch, S. C., & Weiner, B. (2001). A meta-analytic review of coping with illness: Do causal attributions matter? *Journal of Psychosomatic Research, 50*, 205–219.

Roloff, M. E., & Chiles, B. (2011). Interpersonal conflict: Recent trends. In M. Knapp & J. Daly (eds), *The handbook of interpersonal communication* (4th edn, pp. 423–442.). Thousand Oaks, CA: Sage.

Rotter, J. C., & Boveja, M. E. (1999). Counseling military families. *The Family Journal, 7*, 379–382.

Sahlstein, E. (2006). Making plans: Praxis strategies for negotiating uncertainty–certainty in long-distance relationships. *Western Journal of Communication, 70*, 147–165.

Sahlstein, E., Maguire, K. C., & Timmerman, L. (2009). Contradictions and praxis contextualized by wartime deployment: Wives' perspectives revealed through relational dialectics. *Communication Monographs, 76*, 421–442.

Schrodt, P., Witt, P. L., & Messersmith, A. S. (2008). A meta-analytical review of family communication patters and their associations with information processing, behavioral, and psychosocial outcomes. *Communication Monographs, 75*, 248–269.

Scott, J. L., Halford, W. K., & Ward, B. G. (2004). United we stand? The effects of a couple-coping intervention on adjustment to early stage breast or gynecological cancer. *Journal of Consulting & Clinical Psychology, 72,* 1122–1135.

Segrin, C. (2001). Social skills and negative life events: Testing the deficit stress generation hypothesis. *Current Psychology and Research Reviews, 20*(1), 19–35.

Seligman, M. E. P., & Csikszentmihalyi, M. (2000). Positive psychology: An introduction. *American Psychologist, 55,* 5–14.

Selye, H. (1936). A syndrome produced by diverse nocuous agents. *Nature, 138,* 32.

Selye, H. (1975). Confusion and controversy in the stress field. *Journal of Human Stress, 1*(2), 37–44.

Selye, H. (1993). History of the stress concept. In L. Goldberger & S. Breznitz (eds), *Handbook of stress: Theoretical and clinical aspects* (pp. 7–17). New York: Free Press.

Serido, J., Alemeida, D., & Wethington, E. (2004). Chronic stressors and daily hassles: unique and interactive relationships with psychological distress, *Journal of Health and Social Behaviour, 45*(1), 17–33.

Shapiro, A. F., & Gottman, J. M. (2005). Effects on marriage of a psycho-communicative-educational intervention with couples undergoing the transition to parenthood, evaluation at 1-year post intervention. *Journal of Family Communication, 5,* 1–24.

Sherman, A. C., & Simonton, S. (2001). Coping with cancer in the family. *The Family Journal, 9,* 193–200.

Shields, C. G., & Rousseau, S. J. (2004). A pilot study of an intervention for breast cancer survivors and their spouses. *Family Process, 43,* 95–107.

Sillars, A. L., Canary, D., & Tafoya, M. (2004). Communication, conflict, and the quality of family relationships. *Handbook of family communication* (pp. 414–446). Mahwah, NJ: Lawrence Erlbaum Associates.

Silver, M. (2004). *Breast cancer husband: How to help your wife (and yourself) during diagnosis, treatment, and beyond.* Emmaus, PA: Rodale.

Simmons, B. L., & Nelson, D. L. (2001). Eustress at work: The relationship between hope and health in hospital nurses. *Health Care Management Review, 26*(4), 7–18.

Skerrett, K. (1998). Couple adjustment to the experience of breast cancer. *Family Systems and Health, 16,* 281–298.

Skinner, E. A., Edge, K., Altman, J., & Sherwood, H. (2003). Searching for the structure of coping: A review and critique of category systems for classifying ways of coping. *Psychological Bulletin, 129,* 216–269.

Smock, P. J., & Greenland, F. R. (2010). Diversity in pathways to parenthood: Patterns, implications, and emerging research directions. *Journal of Marriage and Family, 72,* 576–593.

Snider, D. M. (1999). The future of American military culture: An uninformed debate on military culture. *Orbis, 43*(1), 11–26.

References

Snyder, C. R. (2002). Hope theory: Rainbows in the mind. *Psychological Inquiry, 13,* 249–275.

Socha, T., & Yingling, J. (2010). *Families communicating with children.* Cambridge, UK: Polity Press.

Soeters, J., Poponete, C., & Page, J. T. (2006). Culture's consequences in the military. In T. Britt, A. Adler, & C. Castro (eds), *Military life: The psychology of serving in peace and combat: Military culture* (Vol. 4) (pp. 13–34). Westport, CT: Praeger Security International; Greenwood Publishing Group.

Solomon, D. S., & Knobloch, L. K. (2004). A model of relational turbulence: The role of intimacy, relational uncertainty, and interference from partners in appraisals of irritations. *Journal of Social and Personal Relationships, 21,* 795–816.

Spitzberg, B. H. (1994). The dark side of (in)competence. In B. Spitzberg & W. Cupach (eds), *The dark side of interpersonal communication* (pp. 25–50). Hillsdale, NJ: Lawrence Erlbaum.

Spitzberg, B. H., & Cupach, W. R. (eds). (1994). *The darkside of interpersonal communication.* Hillsdale, NJ: Lawrence Erlbaum.

Spitzberg, B. H., & Cupach, W. R. (eds). (2007). *The darkside of interpersonal communication.* Hillsdale, NJ: Lawrence Erlbaum.

Splonskowski, J. M., & Twiss, J. J. (1995). Maternal coping adaptations, social support, and transition difficulties to parenthood of first-time civilian and military mothers. *Military Medicine, 160,* 28–32.

Stafford, L. (2005). *Maintaining long-distance and cross-residential relationships.* Mahwah, NJ: Lawrence Erlbaum.

Stamp, G. H. (1994). The appropriation of the parental role through communication during the transition to parenthood. *Communication Monographs, 61,* 89–112.

Stamp, G. H., & Banski, M. A. (1992). The communicative management of constrained autonomy during the transition to parenthood. *Western Journal of Communication, 56,* 281–300.

Stein, M. & Miller, A. H.(1993). Stress, the immune system, and health and illness. In L. Goldberger & S. Breznitz (eds), *Handbook of stress: Theoretical and clinical aspects* (pp. 127–141). New York: Free Press.

Stetz, K. M., Lewis, F. M., & Primomo, J. (1986). Family coping strategies and chronic illness in the mother. *Family Relations, 35,* 515–522.

Sullivan, C. F. (1997). Women's ways of coping with breast cancer. *Women's Studies in Communication, 20,* 59–81.

Taché, J., & Selye, H. (1985). Stress and coping mechanisms. *Issues in Mental Health Nursing, 7,* 3–24.

Thatsum, M., Johansen, M. B., Gubba, L., Olesen, L. B., & Romer, G. (2008). Coping, social relations, and communication: A qualitative exploratory study of children of parents with cancer. *Clinical Child Psychology and Psychiatry, 13,* 123–138.

References

Theiss, J. A., Knobloch, L. K., Checton, M. G., & Magsamen-Conrad, K. (2009). Relationship characteristics associated with the experience of hurt in romantic relationships: A test of the relational turbulence model. *Human Communication Research, 35*, 588–615.

Thoits, P. A. (1991). Gender differences in coping with emotional distress. In J. Eckenrode (ed.), *The social context of coping* (pp. 107–138). New York: Plenum Press.

Thoits, P. A. (1995). Stress, coping, and social support. Where are we? What is next? *Journal of Health and Social Behavior, (extra issue)*, 53–79.

Thompson, S., & O'Hair, H. D. (2008). Advice-giving and the management of uncertainty for cancer survivors. *Health Communication, 23*, 340–348.

Tomlinson, P. S., & Irwin, B. (1993). Qualitative study of women's reports of family adaptation pattern four years following transition to parenthood. *Issues in Mental Health Nursing, 14*, 119–138.

Turner, L. H., & West, R. (2006). *Perspectives on family communication* (3rd edn). Boston: McGraw Hill.

US Army FRG Leader's Handbook (4th edn) (2010). Retrieved May 1, 2010 from www.carlisle.army.mil/usawc/mfp/docs/FRGLeaderHandbook2010.pdf

US Census Bureau (n.d.). *Glossary of terms*. Retrieved September 10, 2010 from http://factfinder.census.gov/home/en/epss/glossary_f.html.

US Census Bureau (2009). *Children characteristics*. Retrieved March 16, 2011 from http://factfinder.census.gov/servlet/STTable?_bm=y&-geo_id=01000US&-qr_name=ACS_2009_5YR_G00_S0901&-ds_name=ACS_2009_5YR_G00_&-redoLog=false&-format=&-CONTEXT=st.

Vangelisti, A. L. (1994). Messages that hurt. In W. R. Cupach & B. H. Spitzberg (eds), *The dark side of interpersonal communication* (pp. 53–82). Hillsdale, NJ: Lawrence Erlbaum.

Vangelisti, A. L., Maguire, K., Alexander, A. L., & Clark, G. (2007). Hurtful family environments: Links with individual and relationship variables. *Communication Monographs, 74*, 357–385.

Vangelisti, A. L., & Young, S. L. (2000). When words hurt: The effects of perceived intentionality on interpersonal relationships. *Journal of Social and Personal Relationships, 17*, 393–424.

Ventura, J. N., & Boss, P. B. (1983). The family coping inventory applied to parents with new babies. *Journal of Marriage and Family, 45*, 867–875.

Wadsworth, S. M. (2010). Family risk and resilience in the context of war and terrorism. *Journal of Marriage and the Family, 72*, 537–556.

Walsh, F. (2003). Family resilience: A framework for clinical practice. *Family Process, 42*, 1–18.

Wang, W., & Morin, R. (2009). Home for the holidays, and every other day. *The Pew Center for Research: Social and Demographic Trends*. Retrieved September 21, 2010 from http://pewsocialtrends.org/2009/11/24/home-for-the-holidays-and-every-other-day/.

References

Wanzer, M., Sparks, L., & Frymier, A. B. (2009). Humorous communication within the lives of older adults: The relationships among humor, coping efficacy, age, and life satisfaction. *Health Communication, 24*, 128–136.

Watzlawick, P., Bavelas, J. B., & Jackson, D. D. (1967). *Pragmatics of human communication: A study of interactional patterns, pathologies, and paradoxes.* New York: Norton.

Weber, K. M., & Solomon, D. H. (2008). Locating relationship and communication issues among stressors associated with breast cancer. *Health Communication, 23*, 548–559.

Weber, K. M., & Solomon, D. H. (2010). Understanding challenges associated with breast cancer: A cluster analysis of intrapersonal and interpersonal stressors. In M. Miller-Day (ed.), *Going through this together: Family communication, connection, and health transitions* (pp. 77–100). New York: Peter Lang.

Werner, E., & Smith, R. (1992). *Overcoming the odds: High risk children from birth to adulthood.* Ithaca, NY: Cornell University.

Wethington, E., & Kessler, R. C. (1991). Situations and processes of coping. In J. Eckenrode (ed.), *The social context of coping* (pp. 13–30). New York: Plenum.

Wheaton, B. (1997). The nature of chronic stress. In B. H. Gottlieb (ed.), *Coping with chronic stress* (pp. 43–74). New York: Plenum.

Wiens, T. W., & Boss, P. (2006). Maintaining family resiliency before, during and after military separation. In C. A. Castro, A. B. Adler, & T. W. Britt (eds), *Military life: The psychology of serving in peace and combat: The military family* (Vol. 3) (pp. 12–38). Westport, CT: Praeger Security International.

Wilcox, B. L. (1986). Stress, coping, and the social milieu of divorced women. In S. Hobfoll (ed.), *Stress, social support, and women* (pp. 115–136). New York: Hemisphere Publishing.

Windle, M., & Windle, R. C. (1996). Coping strategies, drinking motives, and stressful life events among adolescents: Associations with emotional and behavioral problems, and academic functioning. *Journal of Abnormal Psychology, 105*, 551–560.

Wright, K. M., Burrell, L. M., Schroeder, E. D., & Thomas, J. L. (2006). Military spouses: Coping with the fear and the reality of service member injury and death. In C. Castro, A. Adler, & T. Britt (eds), *Military life: The psychology of serving in peace and conflict* (Vol. 3, pp. 64–90). Westport, CT: Praeger Security International.

Yerkes, S. A., & Holloway, H. C. (1996). War and homecomings: The stressors of war and of returning from war. In R. Ursano & A. Norwood (eds), *Emotional aftermath of the Persian Gulf War: Veterans, families, communities, and nations* (pp. 25–42). Washington, DC: American Psychiatric Press.

Young, S. L., Kubicka, T. L., Tucker, C. E., Chavez-Appel, D., & Rex, J. S. (2005). Communicative responses to hurtful messages in families. *Journal of Family Communication, 5*, 123–140.

Index

Index

CanCOPE intervention 134
Carter, B. 152, 156
  and McGoldrick, M. 42, 45
case studies
  breast cancer 139–49

  parenthood 163–73
  wartime deployment 101–2,
    114–25
Castle, H. et al. 154, 160–1
Caughlin, J.
  and Afifi, T. 70
  and Huston, T. 92
causal attribution 40–1
Center for Disease Control, US 127
childcare and birthing classes 161
children
  adult 44–5
  relational stressors in cancer
    diagnosis 132–3
  see also parenthood
chronic stressors 17–18
cognitive appraisals 10–11, 14, 52–3
cognitive coping strategies 59, 93,
  112, 137, 164
Cohen, F. and Lazarus, R. S. 51
communal coping 65–6, 95
communication 26, 55, 89–95
  conversation and conformity
    orientation 87–8
  definition 78–9
  demand/withdrawal pattern 92
  exchange-based model 78
  hurtful 11–12, 82
  as indication of family health and
    functioning 95–6
  as meaning-making 79, 84–6
  oppositional 71–2
  and protective buffering 71, 90–1,
    135–6
  as resource 86–8
  as source or symptom of stress 81–8
  symbolic 78–9
Compas, B. E. et al. 54, 129, 130, 131
conflict 81–3, 91, 92, 96
  see also marital relationships
conformity orientation 87–8

Contextual Model 34–9, 56
conversation orientation 87–8
Coping with Separation Inventory 111
coping/coping strategies
  definitions 50–8
  Double ABC-X model 32, 33
  family as resource 22
  forms 59, 69–72
  functions 60–3
  levels 63–8
  and outcomes 68–74
  breast cancer 136–8
  parenthood 161–3
  wartime deployment 111–25
  paradoxes 72, 90–1
  see also communication
counseling professionals 134, 135
Coyne, J. C.
  et al. 57
  and Fiske, V. 62
  and Smith, D. A. F. 61, 62

Davey, M. et al. 128, 129, 132
DeLongis, A. and O'Brien, T. 57,
  62–3
Donovan-Kicken & Caughlin, J. 88,
  89, 136, 138
demand/withdrawal pattern of
  communication 92
deployment see wartime deployment
developmental stressors 42–5
  and coping 54
discrete stressors 16–17
distress 14–15
Doss, B. D. et al. 155, 156, 157, 158
Double ABC-X model of family crisis
  31–4, 55–6
Drummet, A. R. et al. 106, 108, 109,
  110, 114
Dunivin, K. 103
dyadic/mutual coping 56–8, 133
  negative 138
  parenthood 159–60, 162–3
Dysart-Gale, D. 36

Edwards, J. R. and Cooper, C. L.
  14–15

196

Index

Index